LIVING

LIVING

Inspiration from a Father with Cancer

Jeff Stewart

authorjeffreystewart@gmail.com
Wadsack-Stewart Press

ISBN 979-8-9876691-1-2

For my family in case I can't tell you in person

Contents

A Good Way to Get Bad News

July 11, 2022

This morning I tried to donate my kidney. This afternoon the transplant team told me I can't. I have cancer.

Yes, this is bad news. But I was also lucky. It could have been much worse.

I've been trying for several years to donate. It seemed like the right thing to do. I was rejected a decade ago because of my gastric bypass. Transplant surgeons have since gotten more comfortable with donations from bypass patients. My bypass stopped being a hard barrier at North Carolina, Chapel Hill, which is my nearest transplant center. I was scrutinized before getting a green light: blood tests, urine tests, psych tests, and a kidney ultrasound. I had to fast, then drink a drink so cloying I nearly vomited. I had to lose twenty pounds and get off my high blood pressure meds. That took me almost a year, but I got there.

Then the kidney doc rejected me because I was prediabetic. Frustrating. I tried Georgetown University. They rejected me. I tried Duke. Rejected again. I remember thinking, *It shouldn't be this hard.* Shouldn't donation be an impulse buy? I didn't want to have to be brave more than once. I don't like pain. Each polite *no* was a chance for me to chicken out. But Duke's polite *no* wasn't final.

They would take me if I lost even more weight and got my blood sugar under complete control. Over the next year I dropped another fifty-five pounds and nailed my blood sugar. I came back to Duke. They accepted me as a living kidney donor. I was excited but a little scared. Today I went in for final screening. That screening probably saved my life.

Duke's final donation screen is an abdominal CT scan to confirm I have two kidneys. Some people don't. On that scan, the radiologist found not one but two tumors. One is a renal-cell carcinoma in my right kidney. The other tumor is on the part of my small intestine that's no longer hooked up. This tumor is a duodenal GIST. A GIST is a gastrointestinal stromal tumor. It's a tumor of the cells around my intestines.

That the two tumors are different kinds tells me they are probably unrelated to each other, rather than being one cancer that spread to two places. I know that much from my molecular biology training.

I may, however, have a genetic disease. A genetic disease could cause multiple tumors. I hope I don't have a genetic disease. I wouldn't want my DNA to put my kids at risk. I'm hopeful it's just random chance that I got two different cancers.

This is what's lucky: My tumors would have been vanishingly unlikely to catch without the CT scan. I have no symptoms. Kidney tumors kill because they have no symptoms . . . until it's too late. My intestinal tumor normally would have blocked my digestion or been spotted by a doctor looking down there with an endoscope. But that part of my intestine isn't hooked up. The tumor is in the bypassed parts. I had endoscopy less than a month ago. The doctor saw nothing. Today's CT scan was the only realistic way to find these tumors early. That's the incredible luck to it.

What's next for me? The tumors have to go. That means surgery. I may also need targeted oral chemotherapy. I'm hopeful that I won't need harder, broad-spectrum chemo. If my tumors were really caught as early as I hope, the five-year survival for each is over 93%. I looked it up. My job is to advise life-science companies on new drugs. I know where to find such numbers.

What about the remaining 7%—the part where I don't survive the next five years? I'm fifty years old. I'm not ready to die. Far from it. I have seven kids. My older kids are adults, but my youngest, Annelise, is twelve. I'll have to treat myself as though I were one of my pharma clients. What's the best treatment for my cancer? Is there something better in development? This is the kind of problem I'm used to solving on behalf of others. I'll have to think for myself this time.

My transplant team is handing me off to the surgeons. They will excise my tumors as soon as Duke can schedule things.

Ninety-three-percent odds of surviving the next five years aren't quite as high as those of the average fifty-year-old. They aren't quite as high as I would like. But they aren't bad.

Forgive me. I'm cheating a bit as I write this last part of this first chapter. Three months from now—for reasons that will become clear—I will realize I should write down now what I want my kids to know later. I have gathered up the life lessons, adages, and reflections that helped me endure hard times and avoid harder ones. I am putting these inspirations to paper now in case I'm not there later to say them myself. They are my messages in a bottle. I will toss them into the flood of the future. You've uncorked my bottle. I hope a message you unfurl will help you when you need inspiration. That will be enough.

Inspiration 100

See your good luck.

You'll meet people who mutter about how unlucky they are. Life dumps on them. It's so unfair! These people are unhappy. Worse, they don't learn from their mistakes. If every bad result comes from bad luck, then they never made a mistake in the first place. They can't learn from their mistakes. Nobody can learn to live a life free of bad luck. The way out of this mental trap is to see when we are lucky. Really see it. If we don't fall in love with our own greatness, if we see when our success is merely good luck, we can feel better about our luck sometimes being bad. Bad luck isn't life dumping on us. Bad luck is just the coin coming up tails this time. When we see our good luck, the pupil of our mind's eye dilates. We see things in a different light. We can see when we legitimately earned our success. We learn from earned success. We can also see more clearly why we fail. Sometimes we fail because of bad luck. Other times we fail because we made a mistake. If we can accept our mistakes as mistakes, we can learn from them too.

Inspiration 99

Let the score take care of itself.

In a game of chance, we make the best decisions we know. That's all we can do. Sometimes we flip over the ace. Sometimes we flip over the joker. We aren't winners when we win. We aren't losers when we lose. We are winners when we make the best play. Bad plays are bad plays even when they pay off. Focus on playing your best, not on the final score. Improve by ruthlessly identifying your mistakes—even when you win, especially when you win. Players who obsess over finding the best play win more often. That's what makes them winners in the long run.

A Surgeon for Each Tumor

July 25, 2022

Each of my tumors has its own surgeon. One surgeon's name starts with the letter A. The other's starts with the letter Z. I literally have doctors from A to Z.

Today I saw Dr. A, the urology oncology surgeon. He's the most carefully attired doctor I've ever met. His unusually shaded belt matched his unusually shaded dress shoes. He wore a bow tie. He'll operate on my kidney. He agreed with what I thought last week: The tumors are probably cancer, not some random growths. We probably caught them early. We won't know for sure until after the tumors are out.

Dr. A showed me my tumors on the CT scan. CT means "computed tomography." I know what *computed* means. *Tomography?* Tomography means an image made from a bunch of slices through something. I think of it like the bread with mixed dark and white rye. We can tell the whole shape of the bread by looking at each slice. Or, at least, Dr. A can.

When Dr. A showed me the CT scans of my kidney, I found it hard at first to tell what each blob in the image slices meant. Sure enough, though, my right kidney blob had an oval in the middle, filled with wavy lines that seemed out of place. I later looked these up. The lines are gristly partitions that divide up many kidney cancers as though they were bubble wrap. I don't know if you remember the look of mitochondria from tenth-grade biology, but if you do, my tumor looked like a mitochondrion: same shape, a sausage with all the lines running through it. The look of the tumor is enough to tell Dr. A that mine is probably a renal-cell carcinoma, not a harmless growth.

My intestinal tumor was harder for me to make out. To be honest, that tumor just looked like another blob of intestine to me. I think if you look at normal CT scans for a while the normal parts look normal and the weird parts look weird. It all looked like rye bread to me.

Dr. Z, the gastrointestinal oncology surgeon, will cut out my intestinal tumor, the GIST. Drs. A and Z work a lot together. They do "robotic surgery."

Robotic surgery is scheduled for early September.

They don't actually use robots. It's more like remote control.

Inspiration 98

Unless it's dangerous, dive right in.

All newbies have some dumb ideas. It takes at least some experience to know just how dumb our dumb ideas are. The faster we get in there, the faster we can see why our dumb ideas are dumb. The faster we learn *that*, the faster we can get good ideas. This also goes for creative works. When we start creating right away, we can work through our bad ideas. Dive right in.

If it's dangerous to dive, that's a different story. Don't learn from trial and error not to swim with hungry sharks. When it's dangerous, ask for advice, lower the stakes, take your time.

Inspiration 97

There are good people everywhere. There are bad people everywhere.

I don't care how bad a large group is, there are good people in it. Yes, even that one. Good people may not realize the nature of where they find themselves. Help good people leave bad groups. Helping good people realize they serve a bad cause may be the best thing you can do for them and everyone else.

I don't care how good a large group is, there are bad people in it. Yes, even that one. Predators hide among prey. Help separate bad people from their intended victims. Keeping bad people from the power to harm may be the best thing you can do for them and everyone else.

Road Trip

August 3, 2022

We're on a cross-country road trip to my childhood home in Oregon. The family is split between two minivans. I'm in the one listening to books on tape. The other minivan is playing show tunes. All seven kids plus my bearded son-in-law are self-sorted between the minivans along the audiobook-musical axis.

Yesterday, I tested positive for Covid. Exciting.

It's good timing, all things considered. This gets me through Covid in advance of surgery. At least vaccination lowers my chance of hospitalization by about 90%. I especially need the protection since Covid is about twice as deadly for cancer patients—though I suspect that's also because of chemo. Chemo kills immune system cells along with hair follicles, stomach lining, and cancer.

I started taking Paxlovid today. Getting Paxlovid approved by my insurance is one dubious benefit of having cancer. Access to the drug is reserved for those with serious risk factors. That usually means someone older than I am or sicker than I look. The intake nurse in Santa Fe gave me the standard "Paxlovid is for people with real problems" talking-to. "I have cancer" sort of killed the conversation.

Inspiration 96

The other lanes aren't always faster.

There is a mental illusion that every lane in traffic is going faster than ours. We think the other lanes are faster even when all the lanes run at the same average speed. We cast this illusion on ourselves. While we are stopped, we fume over the passing cars. We count every slow second as if we are being robbed. When our lane moves, we barely notice how many cars we fly past. We remember being passed. Driving past, we forget.

This is true off the highway too. Others seem to be passing us by. Their lives appear to be racing ahead while we are stuck. It's an illusion. Many people post smiling group photos on social media. Few post ugly-cry selfies.

Inspiration 95

A little more speed means a lot more crash.

On long trips, go a bit under the speed limit. It's a different driving experience. The highway stops feeling like NASCAR and starts feeling like the lazy river ride at Sesame Place. The traffic stops being your field of rivals and starts to be the water flowing around you. You become the only raft on your own private drift spot. Try it.

If you see a deer, slow way down. I've hit three deer. The first deer sped up to run straight into the side of our new-to-us car. The second deer stopped walking when I tried to slip behind it. The third deer was the middle one crossing the road. Deer do not make wise traffic decisions. You'll have to do it for them . . . and better than I did.

Straight to IKEA

August 20, 2022

My least favorite thing is moving. My second least favorite thing is shopping. We just dropped off Mallory for her freshman year at UNC Charlotte. Guess what that entailed?

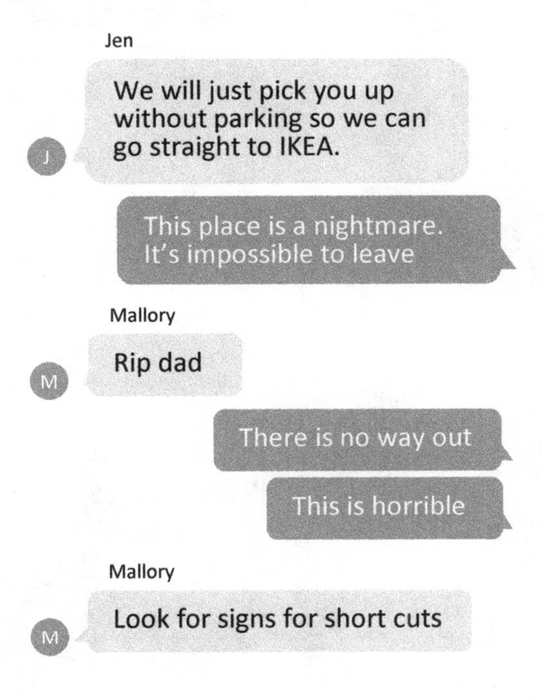

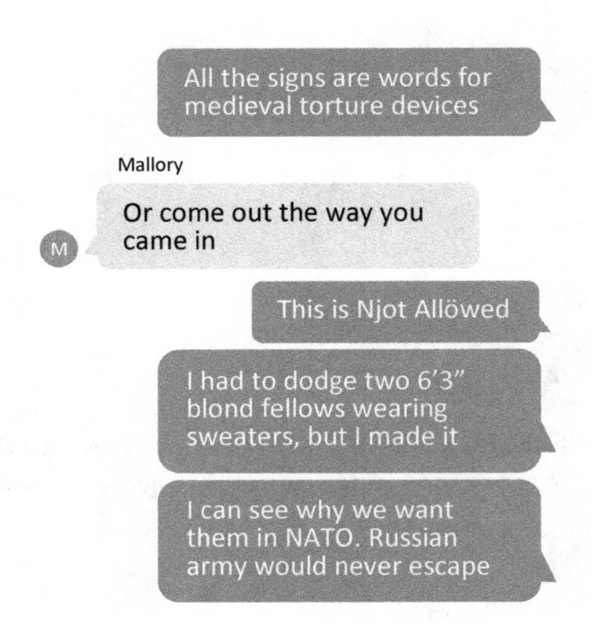

My surgery is in two weeks.

Inspiration 94

Corporations are high-functioning psychopaths.

A body is not a big cell. A swarm is not a big bee. A corporation is not a big person (despite the word's origin). Corporations don't know right from wrong. Corporations do not fear for the souls they do not have. Don't expect corporations to feel remorse. Don't expect corporations to repent of their sins. Corporations are self-interested. Corporations reliably respond to one thing and one thing only: consequences. If corporations were people, they would be psychopaths. Yes, there can be honorable company leaders who do the right thing despite shareholder interests. Sooner or later, shareholders replace those leaders with ones who raise the stock price by taking profits more honorable leaders would not. This is why corporate regulation is so important. Regulation clears an ethical space where company leaders can act like human beings.

Don't get me wrong. I admire many corporations. Corporations get things done. Just don't expect corporations to be what they're not.

Inspiration 93

Crowds are idiot savants.

There is wisdom in crowds. There is also mass insanity. The trick is to know when to trust crowds and when to scamper to safety. Crowds can be savants at finding the right answer when everyone works independently on a problem. How heavy is the ox? A crowd will nail that one within a few pounds. It's when crowds lose independent judgment, when they start group work, that crowds can turn into idiots. Crowds that follow idiots will be idiots. Crowds can be led astray.

Nothing Bad Better Happen

September 2, 2022

Love you all. I can't promise things will go well tomorrow, but the odds are very, very good. If, for some reason, things go very badly, know I love you all and am honored to be in your family

Jordan

J

Love you too! And nothing bad better happen! And we will visit you when you are not cranky

Jessica

J

Well, you can think about it this way—you already have the risk and they are removing it from you. You can only get safer

Inspiration 92

The scaffolding must come down once the building is up.

We always hope we are building the final structure. We put our all into something. We hope it will last. We finally see the shape of a building, and we at first think we are done. Often, we are not done. What we mistook for a finished building was only scaffolding. When we see that the scaffolding is scaffolding, we realize we have more work to do. All the scaffolding work we have done, none of it can stay. It all has to come down. This can be discouraging. Remember that the scaffolding is not the building. You needed the scaffolding. You had to put the scaffolding up for the building to go up. It's part of the process. Once the building is up, the scaffolding must come down.

Inspiration 91

Take stock of what you've built.

When you get something built, stop for a moment. Take in what you've made. Sign the painting. Frame the diploma. Stand back. It's no sin to take pride in a job done right. Seeing what we've built, really taking it in, sets a tile in our personal mosaic. When the tile is set, we don't have to fuss with it. We don't have to relive the past. We build on it. We see a bit more of the picture. We see the next tile to lay.

I Can Start from the Beginning, Right?

My bearded son-in-law: *I'm doing interviews with, for lack of a better term, old people.*

So why am I on this?

This recording? I guess for your sake it was more of, not to be morbid, but, you know, your recent condition. I thought this would be a good kind of chronicling, archiving of just all the stuff you want to talk about of your life until now. If your kids want to listen to us down the line, they can hear all the stuff that happened.

I can start from the beginning, right?

I was born in 1972 in The Dalles, Oregon. The Dalles at the time was the biggest town for nearly one hundred miles—all the way to Portland to the west, and even farther to the east. We were the big town, but the big town was only ten thousand people. If you've played the game *Oregon Trail*, you stopped in The Dalles to decide to take the Barlow Road or float down the Columbia River.

I didn't realize it was in the Oregon Trail *game. Little bit of trivia, I guess.*

It's small-town America. Cherry orchards and wheat fields surround it. The last miles where Portland rain still showers down are just out of sight, around the river bend. From The Dalles east to the Mississippi, it's dry. The Dalles is where flyover country begins.

My mom and dad both started as schoolteachers. My mom taught me to read. She also raised me on *The Diary of Anne Frank* and Corrie ten Boom's *The Hiding Place*. She set my moral compass.

My dad's weird career taught me the courage to try different things. He grew up in Mount Vernon, Oregon, population five hundred. As he tells it, when people heard that a kid from Mount Vernon was planning on going to college, they laughed. He taught for a few years, which kept him out of Vietnam. He met my mom at the school where they both taught. My dad didn't love teaching or school administration and left to be his own boss—general contracting, buying and fixing rental houses, holding a semi-permanent yard sale, running our small farm. This wasn't enough to make ends meet, so even though he hated doing it, my dad got a job at the aluminum plant.

The aluminum plant was the real driver of the economy. The plant was the good job in town. It was shift work. The plant was in The Dalles because the electricity on the Columbia River was cheap. So was the shipping. The factories are now gone—I mean completely gone, not just shut down. They were carted away for scrap. The cheap hydropower is now sold to Bitcoin miners and Google. But of course, those don't employ the people the aluminum plant did.

In the 1980s, the economy went south. The plant started layoffs. That was a shock. The layoffs created in me a sense of unrest that things wouldn't always necessarily be all that good economically. I've never shaken it. I think it's been to my good. It makes me empathize with people who aren't doing so well. My dad got laid off. As part of his severance, my dad got a business loan and built an auto radiator repair shop. That shop became the main family business. The shop is still there, next to the house.

My parents were hard workers, still are. My dad is in his seventies, and he still works harder than anyone I know. My mom substitute-teaches and does social work. I worked with my dad in the radiator shop, in rental houses, and on the farm. I worked with my mom in the house. They taught me to work hard.

My mother's mother semi-lived with us. She cleaned our house. She was a widow, and she needed the money because whatever she could spare she would send to Jimmy Swaggart and Jim and Tammy Faye Bakker. You could always tell where my grandmother was in the house. The nearest TV was set to the Trinity Broadcasting Network at the highest volume. When I later saw grifters raising money from people who couldn't afford it, I knew it for what it was. I had seen it before. Evil dresses nice. Evil wears makeup.

We, my two younger sisters and I, grew up in the house that my dad built. While we grew up together, I don't know how much we were on the same page. Angie was far more socially with it than I ever have been. She's a PhD psychologist now. Amy and I butted heads. If I was playing a board game, I was playing that game by myself in my room. Or I was reading a book. I always, always, always was reading a book. My mom, as a teacher, was maybe overinvested in me as a child. Early on she was doing word flashcards with me. I had the alphabet memorized and started to read before I was two. I don't know where I'd be without my mom doing that. I just don't know. As it was, it worked. I was smart, and I liked it. I didn't mind telling you how smart I thought I was.

School in The Dalles was always easy for me. I didn't have a 4.0 GPA, but that was because I was kind of obnoxious at times. I got myself suspended my freshman year when I took wires and stuck them in an outlet and blew the circuit with a bang. I did it because I thought the teacher was stupid. That was not a smart way to retaliate. That teacher gave me the *B* that blew my perfect GPA. My senior year I raised a stink about the old grade, and he came up with a secret grade book supposedly documenting my lack of participation points. I don't think the ink was dry on the "zero" entries for me three years after that class.

I almost never took homework home. That ended up annoying the chemistry teacher. He gave my class a test where none of the material was covered in the lectures and all of it was in the textbook he knew I hadn't read. That's not paranoia. He told me later why he did it. He did it to teach me a lesson. My face must have been completely punchable.

Choir was a formative experience for me. The choir teacher was able to draw excellence from us. We were the best choir in the state. It was fantastic. I think it's important to have one thing as a child where you perform at the highest level you can. That one experience resonates through life. When things are bad, you remember being the best at something.

One thing I wasn't the best at was acting. I acted in several plays. I liked it. I felt at the time the director didn't much like me though. There aren't a lot of high school guys who can sing and act. When we put on *Seven Brides for Seven Brothers*, the director found me not good enough to be one of those seven. I think the non-validation of my acting pushed me to seek the spotlight. I did community theater for years. I now host the podcast at our publicly traded company.

The high school academic experience that mattered the most to me was the trivia team. Oh, my gosh, did I love playing trivia. I didn't realize it at the time—we didn't keep score in practice—but I was made to play trivia. That year at states, if I wasn't the highest scorer, I was close to it. We won every game I was in. Coaches from the Portland teams remarked on it. We won state the next two years. That's how I got to believe I could win on *Jeopardy!*

I tried out for *Teen Jeopardy!* My dad drove us the six hours to Boise to try out. I lost, which was a disappointment. It was good luck that I didn't pass the *Jeopardy!* audition as a teen. I needed the time in college to get good enough to play against the adults I'd later face in the Tournament of Champions.

Childhood wasn't all good. I was bullied in middle school. One bully was from church, and the other was a tenor sax player from jazz band. I think kindly of most people. I had a tough time forgiving my bullies. Whenever I picture them, I still tense for the punch. Somehow, I'm still afraid of the sax player even though he's been dead for years. I know, now, that his father was an abuser—beatings, cigarette burns.

I didn't date much at all in high school. I think, as I look back, I just knew something was missing. No girl clicked with me the way I somehow knew I needed. It made me wonder if I'd ever find someone.

Someone who did click with me was my friend Robert. Up to that point, people didn't seem as if they were like me. They just weren't. The arrogant way to say it would be—

They couldn't keep up?

They couldn't keep up. At least that's how I saw it then. I was intolerant. The truer way to say it is we weren't on the same wavelength. But Robert? With Robert, it was a satisfying click the way a padlock clicks with the right key. We would immediately pick up on what the other was saying. We read the same science fiction books. We played the same games. We were in the same math and science classes. Any time we were in a class, we would sit next to each other and talk, sometimes while the teacher lectured. We would talk and talk and talk. I didn't realize it then, but my friendship with Robert set the bar for what I needed in a girlfriend. I needed someone with whom I could just talk. I didn't meet any girl who really did that until I met Jen. She ended up being my only girlfriend and later my wife.

I first felt discrimination when I applied to be an Eagle Scout. The Eagle Board of Review had members who were known around town for having a beef with my religion. Among other things, they said I needed to repeat my leadership positions in another scout troop—in another church, not my church. They said I had to accept their ruling or risk never getting the Eagle rank I had worked toward since I was eight. I remember driving home and thinking, and this is the kind of thinking a teenager has, I should wrap my car around a tree and really show them how hurtful what they did was. My scout leader appealed for me. I got assigned a new board and was awarded the Eagle. I was later told my first board members got banned from Eagle boards for life. The whole thing awakened me to discrimination. So had the visiting preacher who told kids my age not to be friends with Mormons. It wasn't much discrimination compared to what Muslims, Blacks, Jews, or immigrants face. It was just a taste. That taste is still in my mouth.

Those are the things I think about when I think about my childhood. These are the things that, looking back, mattered most in making me who I am now.

Inspiration 90

If you really want to learn something, teach it.

We think we know a subject until we try to teach it to others. When we try to teach, we are forced to put things in simple terms. It's only when we put things in simple terms that we really understand them. Our minds can play around with simple things. We see connections we couldn't see before. Your students will see logic holes in what you teach. You won't be able to hide. You'll be forced to fill your gaps. Teaching is the most effective way to learn.

Inspiration 89

Pick the teacher, not the class.

Good teachers make us love life. Bad teachers make us hate the next ninety minutes. Any time you have the chance to learn from a good teacher, take the class. It doesn't matter what the subject is.

Minus the Tumor

September 3, 2022

Jen

First part of surgery just completed: the gastrointestinal stromal tumor (GIST) has been successfully removed as well as the gastric bypassed stomach and a portion of Dad's duodenum because the tumor was too infiltrated within them. His remaining stomach still connects to the jejunum as it did after the gastric bypass. The duodenum end that was cut has been stitched up, and the gallbladder and pancreas feed into the duodenum now later on past the portion that was removed. The next doctor is starting the kidney tumor removal now. Dad seems to have tolerated the surgery well so far.

J

Jen

The second doctor just removed the small kidney tumor. Everything looked good with the rest of the kidney, so he was able to keep that kidney, minus the tumor. Dad is still asleep and not into the recovery room yet, so I haven't seen him.

The doctor said he did very well throughout the whole surgery. Nothing was unexpected except the GIST extending inside the duodenum and outward to the stomach. They couldn't tell that from the CT scan, although such a thing was possible, and I think they knew it was possible. They were hoping they could just lop off the tumor from the outside of the duodenum. But instead they took out the segment of the duodenum to which the tumor had been attached, they also took out the bypassed portion of his stomach too. The kidney tumor removal sounded very straightforward, and that surgery was much shorter—like 1.5 hours versus the 3.5 hours for the other one.

J

After surgery, I wrote this note on my phone to the attending night physician. Talking hurt too much.

> Here is what is going on. Deep or even medium breaths are excruciating (nine on the pain scale). The pain is triggered by moving my intercostal muscles. Being in the wrong position is also excruciating. It's a deep pain. But what is terrible is when one breath is painful leading to the next being a bit more of an inhale, etc.
>
> What I am doing is finding an awkward position that doesn't cause this pain and breathing shallowly. My arms have to be in the right position, or it stretches my wound, and it's nine on a ten scale for pain.
>
> The pain that causes me to ask for meds is related. It's upstream and downstream, both. The odd positions I am choosing are causing a back spasm. I can point you to the specific muscle. It's progressing right now as I hold myself in position. Eventually, I cannot tolerate the back pain and have to reposition or try to release the spasm using the press-and-hold method.
>
> This repositioning is excruciating and triggers the deeper breathing, which is excruciating, and so on.
>
> That's why I requested a muscle relaxant. This did not, unfortunately, release the spasm.
>
> What I do know that can release a muscle spasm is a massage. I think PT should be well aware of how this works. Or if you have a chiropractor in the hospital, that's their wheelhouse. I have never gone to a chiropractor in my entire life, but right now I think it could stop this particular pain cycle.

The hospital had no chiropractor to release my muscle spasm. The attending physician did it, for which I am grateful.

They pumped CO2 into my abdomen so they could put in their little robotic tools and drive them around with some space

The CO2 mostly deflated out. But not all of it. The gas got trapped in each of the tissue layers. The gas migrated up. Now it's collecting in my neck and shoulders. When I rub my skin, it's like tiny bubble wrap. I move my jaw, and I hear pops. Not kidding

Bubbles under my neck and along my clavicle

And on top of my shoulders

Jordan

Yikes

J That sounds scary to me. I'm guessing it isn't dangerous though?

Docs say it's normal

I can make my chest squeak like a rubber duck

Patrick

P That's weird i hope it doesnt hurt?

Surgery was a success. Dr. A removed the kidney tumor without a problem. Dr. Z had to remove part of my stomach and small intestine, but both were already bypassed. Recovery from this surgery is hard for most people since new digestion is a major lifestyle change. Not for me. I had this digestion change a decade ago when I had my bypass surgery.

The surgery left me with five incisions across my gut. It looks like a giant claw grabbed me, then decided *nah*.

Inspiration 88

Identify your scope of influence.

The world's problems can seem so big that we don't know what to do. It can be overwhelming. First, identify your scope of influence. What problems can you make better? Those are the problems you can think about solving. A problem outside your scope of influence might as well be on the moon. You can't fix that problem. Recognize which problems are in your scope of influence. Worry about solving those. There will be plenty.

Inspiration 87

Life is a long first draft.

Writing is not writing. Writing is drafting and editing. We take our first shot in a draft. Then we edit. The first draft is always bad. Editing corrects our errors and builds up our best parts. Editing is at least half the work of writing.

We don't think of life as edited. The past doesn't come with a backspace key. We have to keep writing one long first draft. We filled past pages with a lot of bad prose. The dialogue was awful. The characters were thin. The plot had no purpose. Don't sweat it. Everyone else wrote a bad first draft too. If we are honest, we also see the writing that worked, the phrase that sang, the character we identified with, the page we wanted to turn to read what happens next.

How do we keep our life's work from being a penny dreadful? We have to learn to edit as we write. We re-read the book of our life. We learn from it. We try not to make old errors on a fresh page. We expand on our best parts. We choose our words. We build character. We craft our story with the end in mind.

You're Leaving?

September 4, 2022

Will likely get my discharge today—whenever convenient up to midnight

Jordan

Hey! So I think we are wanting to pick you up soon

They still haven't done discharge paperwork. I'll let you know when I'm legal

Discharge paperwork is in

"It's important for you to walk, Mr. Stewart."

"How many laps today, Mr. Stewart?"

"Yeah, you can just walk. Nobody needs to be with you. It's great you're walking."

"You're leaving? Whatever you do, don't walk! We will get you a wheelchair."

The pathology report will take a week. Then we will know if there is any commonality between my tumors or if it was just one of those things that I got two tumors at the same time. Plus, we will see if my tumor type tells whether I should be taking newer, targeted chemotherapy that doesn't have the same side effects as traditional, broad-based chemo. I'm scared of traditional chemo. The side effects are harsh. I'm not looking forward to targeted chemotherapy either, but at least it's not traditional chemo.

Inspiration 86

Take a walk.

A daily walk helps us think. A daily walk improves our mood. A daily walk can ease depression. A daily walk can seem too simple. It's not. Take a walk.

Inspiration 85

Decline dominance fights with teens.

We want our teenagers to grow up. For teenagers to grow up, they must escape the natural dominance of their parents. To learn about dominance, watch some reruns of *The Dog Whisperer*. Teens can't tolerate being tied too tightly. Only we parents can choose to let go. The only way a teen might know how to get loose is to bite the hand that holds the leash. Teens say hurtful things. See that for what it is. We have to stop clinging to the dominance we held when our kids were just kids. We have to let out some rope. Then we have to let go. We have to learn to be the mentors our teens need us to be as they become the adults they are meant to be.

Cancer on Easy Mode

September 19, 2022

I'm still waiting on my pathology report. Here's what I will be looking for:

Cancerous versus benign tumors. Both tumors are most likely cancerous. But if one tumor or both turn out to be benign, it's not as if the surgeons will put the benign tumors back.

Margins, AKA, "Did they get it all?" The less likely outcome would be bad margins. Bad margins might mean more surgery to get the rest, I would think.

Specific genetic profile. Depending on the genetics of my tumors, different drugs will work better. The most likely outcome is that the kidney tumor doesn't require additional treatment. My kidney tumor was the size of a pink elementary school pencil eraser. It's overwhelmingly likely to be gone-gone. My intestinal tumor, the GIST, should respond to newer, targeted chemotherapy. Most GISTs do. Targeted chemotherapy is not nearly as hard to live with as regular chemo. I guess I might also find out I have genes that make me cancer-prone. That would mean more monitoring, I would think.

My incisions are almost completely healed. The most bothersome thing about recovery was the surgical CO_2 the doctors pumped into me. That gas got into *all* sorts of places. "Pneumoscrotum" is even less sexy than it sounds. It was like a half-full water balloon. It hurt to walk. Dr. A insisted this was normal. (Really?) Dr. A told me to wear supportive underwear. He seemed not to have a ton of sympathy for my plight. I get the feeling complications after cancer surgery tend to be more serious than balloon-balls. The cheapest supportive underwear at Target was a playset of brightly colored thongs. Now I have a drawer full. I'm ready to dress up as a Chippendale dancer this Halloween.

So far this has been cancer on "easy mode." I feel kind of embarrassed about how easy it's been.

Inspiration 84

Defuse the body-image time bomb.

It is a truth universally acknowledged that anyone in possession of a perfectly good body must be in want of a better one. I think everyone has poor body image. Nobody's immune. We can't completely protect our loved ones from poor body image, but we can help. I think it's all about lowering the pressure. To defuse the body-image bomb in you kids, I tried not to criticize my own body, your mother's, or yours. I tried to teach you that being physically attractive is nice in the way that experiencing a warm summer's day is nice. It's a nice experience when it happens. It doesn't define you. I've also tried to teach you that physical attraction comes with downsides. Physically attractive people aren't always taken seriously. Just ask your mother. The beautiful attract the shallow, so it can be harder to find a good match. I think seeing the downsides of physical beauty helps us obsess a bit less.

Inspiration 83

Having not enough money hurts. So does having too much.

It's stressful to have not enough money. When we don't have quite enough, we worry and worry and worry. Earning enough so we don't have to live paycheck to paycheck eases the heart. Having not enough money to invest in ourselves costs us in the end. We don't get the schooling that would make us valuable employees. We don't fix the grinding brakes on the car while the repair's still cheap. We don't get dental checkups. We eat fast food. It's expensive to be poor, as the saying goes. Having enough is worth a lot.

Having more than enough doesn't make us much happier. Even worse, too much money can make us jerks. Drivers of expensive cars stop less often for pedestrians. Really. In one psychological study, the upper class more often stole candy clearly labeled for kids. There is something about having too much money that can make us bad. Puts tithing in a different light, doesn't it?

$25,000 and a Car

Bearded son-in-law: *Did you start college right after high school?*

I went to Brigham Young University. It was the first time I lived outside The Dalles. My graduating class at The Dalles was 150. The university had 28,000, almost three times the population of my whole hometown.

I took a huge course load, like, a crazily large load of classes. It was at least twenty-one credit hours. Maybe it was twenty-four. I was unwise. One of the classes was linear algebra, and I remember my first test. I must have gotten a *C*-, which was embarrassing to me. That class was hard. So were physics, genetics, and organic chemistry. I took them all at the same time. I hadn't developed the chops for keeping good notes. I was used to sitting there and absorbing the material. I'd hear it, and I had it. That was not possible with my college classes. I learned to work for my grades.

BYU had a serious trivia team. I tried out and made the intercollegiate team as a freshman. I was so excited. Apparently, there was a cute, short, smart senior at the tryouts. Her name was Jennifer. She looked younger than a college senior. She was regularly mistaken for being fifteen. I was so focused on making the team, I wasn't really paying a lot of attention to much of anyone else.

She paid attention to me though. "There was something about you," she would later tell me.

The BYU trivia team was a traveling team. We had a big budget. We ate meals on a per diem. We flew to tournaments. We were effectively a varsity sports team but nerds. I remember flying to Georgia Tech, Minnesota, Boston University, Michigan, Illinois, George Washington University, and Florida. We drove the twelve hours to Stanford, the closest major tournament.

I just loved trivia. Trivia always stuck with me. I liked learning it even when it wasn't for a purpose. On the team, trivia had a purpose. The next four years was the difference between playing pick-up basketball and being an NBA prospect.

Ready to be drafted.

Just like that. After four years of serious play, you've heard trivia canon so many times it's just hitting the ball over the net, hitting the ball over the net, hitting the ball over the net. Countries and capitals. Years and presidents. Authors and their works. It's muscle memory at a certain point. Play seriously for four years, and there are few reasonable trivia questions you won't have heard already. You'll have heard variants of the question probably ten times. More.

I wasn't the only one leveled up by the team. Roughly half of us eventually appeared on *Jeopardy!* Ken Jennings, who won the most money in *Jeopardy!* history and is now the show's host, made the team after I graduated.

My first semester on the team, I did not take notice of Jennifer. This was not because she was unattractive. This was not because I didn't like her. I mistakenly thought she was seriously dating—possibly engaged to—another team member. So I wasn't trying to make anything happen. While I wasn't making anything happen, Jennifer was maneuvering. I didn't know, because I was dumb that way. She tried to sit next to me on the flight back from Minneapolis. I moved to an open seat. Yeah, dumb. One night she invited a group over for *Trivial Pursuit.* She skunked me. She was the first person ever to beat me at *Trivial Pursuit.* That got my attention. We ended up being the last ones there. It turned out she wasn't engaged. She was not even dating. Well, okay, then.

Jennifer became my first and last girlfriend. With Jennifer, it's not the same, but similar to the way that Robert and I just could talk. Jen and I just can talk, have conversations, not slow down. This doesn't mean we're the same, because there are a lot of things she knows and a lot of things I don't, and vice versa. But you didn't think you were just going to have the ball dropped, somehow. You knew they would get it, and even if they didn't get the reference, they would be able to keep up. That was a revelation. That was really, really attractive to me.

The summer after my freshman year, we decided to get married. I thought it was a good decision, and I was happy to be with her. She was so smart. She was also kind. You know the after-school specials that have one popular girl who is kind and befriends the outcasts? That girl is Jen. She does that. There is confidence in her kindness. She doesn't care what other people might think of her for being a friend to the friendless. That also attracted me.

Jen gave up a lot, career-wise, to be married to me. She had been accepted into what was then the top law school in the nation, Columbia. She would, I'm sure, have had a lucrative legal career in Manhattan had she chosen differently. But she didn't. She chose me.

Jen went into graduate English. I majored in molecular biology. I thought it was cool. You don't get a lot of work in labs as an undergrad, so you don't really know what molecular biology is like in practice. You just know what the study of molecular biology is like. Those are two different things. That really came back to bite me, but that's for later.

Jen and I played trivia together all the time. We were the trivia couple. The rest of school was fine, but I felt the way many college athletes feel. The school is almost incidental to the sport.

By the summer of my senior year, we had two kids, Jordan and Patrick. Life was not easy at all. I loved being a father. Kids are great. But it wasn't easy. Not a lot of sleep. Not a lot of money.

We totaled our station wagon. My dad said, "Well, what's your plan for getting a new car?"

"I'm going to try out for *Jeopardy!* this semester," I said. I had already sent in fifty postcards to the audition drawing.

My dad paused. I could almost hear the incredulous stare through the apartment phone. "What's the real plan, Jeff?" he said.

One of my fifty postcards was selected. I went to Los Angeles to try out for College *Jeopardy!* I took the written test. You have to get thirty-five of the fifty questions right to move on. They don't tell you your score, but I knew before being told that I had passed. I felt as though I were shooting layups. I was a different player from when I was a teen. I knew practically everything. Then the contestant coordinators gave us a buzzer test.

They're really trying to figure out whether or not you'll look good on the show?

Do you answer questions quickly? Do you have a problem speaking? Do you look good on camera? I'm not saying that it's a beauty contest. But it kind of is one.

It's a show.

It's a show. I got up there and started answering. I was fast on the buzzer and clearly better than the other students. Soon a contestant coordinator said, "Okay, that's enough from Jeff. You can sit down." Then when the other players didn't know their answers, the coordinator asked me what the others had missed. I still remember one of those. "This birthstone was named because it resembled the seeds of a pomegranate." "What is garnet?"

I thought the show producers would think a married student with two kids was either cool or not cool. That's what would determine if I was going to be on the show, really. My gameplay was good.

That fall we got the FedEx from Merv Griffin Studios, Jeopardy Productions, Hollywood and Vine. I was going to represent BYU on the tenth annual *Jeopardy!* College Championship. Then it was just study, study, study.

Jen, two kids, and I flew to L.A. to play *Jeopardy!* They put us up in Merv Griffin's hotel. Merv Griffin was the creator and producer of *Jeopardy!* He made his fortune from it. Jen and I were at his Hilton, the Beverly Hilton. Tommy Lasorda, the manager of the Dodgers, was walking around the lobby. We passed by Sidney Poitier. Jen rode the elevator with the inventor of CGI as he held the Oscar he had just won in the hotel ballroom. It was a ritzy place for somebody like me.

I don't know how much you want to hear about the show itself, but I'll tell you the things that stuck with me. I soaked my hands in hot water in the bathroom outside the green room. As part of *Jeopardy!* study, Jen and I had watched the movie *Thirty Two Short Films About Glenn Gould*. Gould, the piano player, soaked his hands before concerts to limber up his fingers. So I did that before each show. The studio was cold, and I wanted my reaction times to be as fast as humanly possible. I filled the sink with hot water, as hot as I could take it, and soaked.

I don't even know how anyone beats a returning champion. It seems almost impossible because the buzzer system is so whacked. You have to time it just right to get in. If you're too early, you're shut out. If you're too late, you lose. You have to time it perfectly. The timing was based on the speaking cadence of the host, Alex Trebek. When Alex was done speaking, a hidden crew member would flip the switch that turned on the hand buzzers. You get your finger in sync with that hidden switch, and you're absolutely going to destroy somebody who isn't in sync.

I wasn't good on the buzzer at the beginning of the first round. That's the most dangerous time for a new player. You're worried that you're going to look stupid in front of millions of people on television. You're tense. It took time for me to loosen up. But after the first commercial break, if I wanted a question, I pretty much got it. This is unusual. I had a high get-rate. I rolled.

I also got lucky on my first show. I had a near miss. There was one clue where the correct response could only be the half-wolf White Fang or the dog Buck, both from the Jack London novels. I thought it was Buck. I had read *Call of the Wild* probably twenty times as a kid. I rang in but got beaten. I knew the answer cold, and I got beaten. It was a $1,000 clue. But the thing was, I was wrong. My red-headed opponent from the University of Illinois answered, "Buck." Buck was wrong. I rang in and said, "White Fang." That $2,000 swing let me win safely. That could have gone the other way. I might have been one-and-done if I hadn't been beaten to that buzzer.

I try to notice my good luck. I think it helps keep me on an even keel.

I dominated the rest of the tournament. I did screw up the Final Jeopardy math in the final round. If my opponents had gotten it right and I had gotten it wrong, then I would've lost. Alex Trebek razzed me about it after the taping. But I got Final Jeopardy right, so it didn't matter. After Alex announced I won, Jen joined me on stage to kiss me and help pick out our new red Dodge Dakota.

That was a weird feeling walking out of the studio. I had just won on *Jeopardy!* I was the *Jeopardy!* College Champion. I had won twenty-five thousand bucks and a new car. I won the car that we didn't have. It was wonderful.

The championship came with a trophy. It broke when I dropped it the first week back at school. I let the kids keep the heavy glass globe from it as a toy. It made me happy to think of them rolling it around, not knowing what it was. I think it's under Aidan's bed.

How many games of Jeopardy! *did you play?*

Nine. I was on four times for the college tournament: quarterfinal, semifinal, and the two-game final. After that I was on the Tournament of Champions. That was the big league. That was four more games. I scrubbed out of the *Jeopardy!* Ultimate Tournament of Champions. That was game nine.

The summer of 1994, we moved to Princeton. I had three grad schools I could have chosen. I picked, I think, the worst one for me. I got into Chicago, Johns Hopkins, and Princeton. Princeton was close to Jen's family in New Jersey. That mattered. She got to spend more time with her family, including a younger brother who would die an untimely death ten years later.

We moved in with Jen's family two years later when I got kicked out of Princeton.

Inspiration 82

Nobody is ready to be married.

Marriage is a big deal. It's not to be entered into lightly. Don't let that stop you. No matter when we marry, we still will have a lot of growing to do. I've enjoyed getting my growth hand-in-hand with your mother. The psychologist David Schnarch called marriage a "people-growing machine." He compared marriage to well-paired Olympic athletes in training. One spouse will pull ahead in maturity. The other spouse will be forced to catch up or risk being left behind. The couple grows together. Are you ready for that?

Inspiration 81

Don't confuse falling in love with being in love.

Falling in love feels like nothing else. When I say falling in love feels like nothing else, I mean *nothing* else. That includes the feeling of *being* in love. Forming the pair bond comes with its own mix of hormones. Being in love feels different from falling in love. The feeling of falling in love always fades. Expect that. Nothing is going wrong when this happens. Once you are secure in your relationship, you don't have to be driven together by your hormones. The pair-bonding hormones go away. Your relationship is not dead because the falling-in-love feeling is gone. Being in love is a different feeling. Mix the two feelings up at your peril.

Not Cancer on Easy Mode

September 23, 2022

> Pathology collected 9/2/2022 11:00 AM
>
> Status: Edited Result - FINAL
>
> Visible to patient: Yes (seen)
>
> A diffuse type gastric adenocarcinoma, which was not appreciated grossly, involves the entire wall of the stomach.

It's not cancer on easy mode after all. I got my pathology report back. It's not good. It's not a death sentence, but it does mean traditional broad-based chemo and uncertainty.

The good part: My kidney tumor is gone (probably). There is a 99% chance that one's done.

My stomach cancer is bad news in four ways. First, it's not one tumor but two. It's unclear why there are two, if one is birthed by the other one or what. Set that aside. The second way my stomach cancer is bad news is that Dr. Z didn't get it all. The third way is the big one. My stomach cancer is not a GIST-type, which would have responded well to targeted oral chemotherapy. My stomach cancer is a deadly adenocarcinoma. This type of cancer requires hard-core chemo and has a poor prognosis so far as I can tell. Fourth, my gastric adenocarcinoma has spread to at least one lymph node.

Will my gastric cancer kill me sometime in the next five years? It's a coin flip—assuming I'm reading the path report right.

I will have to talk to a new doctor—a medical oncologist—before I know expected treatment, more accurate survival odds, and my expected quality of life. I just don't know.

I can deal with this sort of thing dispassionately. I'm more worried about worrying my family. But if you notice that I am flakier than I used to be, you're probably not wrong.

September 27, 2022

Carissa

C

Really, no more Breaking Bad for you

I'm 95% recovered from surgery. My five small scars are the only signs that anything was cut out.

I had a follow-up this morning with Dr. Z, the gastrointestinal surgeon. If he had known the type of cancer I had, he wouldn't have operated. He would have sent me straight to traditional broad-based chemo. Surgery doesn't usually cure my cancer. It spreads too easily. Given that Dr. Z did operate, he should have removed more lymph nodes for my type of cancer (I looked this up). I found a reference that showed that taking out more lymph nodes improves survival over chemo alone for my cancer. But of course, Dr. Z didn't know I had my cancer. He had thought I had a GIST and took out the right number of lymph nodes for the wrong cancer.

One of the deficiencies in my pathology report was what was supposedly left behind. The report seems to say they missed something (a so-called "positive margin"). A way to think about a positive margin is like the peanut butter in a sandwich. If you took a knife and cut away a bunch of the bread and then looked at all the edges of the cut bread, if you ever saw peanut butter, you know you didn't get it all. That's a positive margin. In reading the path report carefully, it doesn't say where that positive margin is. My intestine? My pancreas? My bypassed stomach remnant Dr. Z removed? My remaining stomach? Dr. Z thought the positive margin most likely was in the middle of a line of surgical staples. These were the staples left from cutting my bypassed stomach remnant in half during removal. That staple line cannot be read by pathology. Dr. Z thinks there wasn't anything left behind. He's following up with the path lab.

I asked if I needed more surgery. Dr. Z thought it unlikely that there would be another surgery in the near term. Chemo is the mainstay for my kind of cancer. If a second surgery had complications, that would slow down my getting chemo.

Most everything will turn now to the medical oncologist. I still need to get the right medical oncologist. The one I'm set up to talk to next week is not the right one. The one I'm scheduled to see specializes in bladder cancer, which is the wrong type of cancer. I need a gastric-cancer specialist.

The major things I am looking to understand from the medical oncologist include what stage my cancer is at, what my prognosis is, what my treatment plan is, what additional imaging I need, and what clinical trials look promising. Dr. Z took a pass on answering any of that, even staging. Stage—a number that roughly says how advanced a cancer has become—he doesn't know, since it could be stage II or III, depending on how many lymph nodes were cancerous. Stage III would be worse. He took out too few lymph nodes to have a clear idea of what stage I'm at because of the whole GIST/adenocarcinoma mix-up.

Cancer stage is important. Cancer type plus stage tells us what treatments are approved and what outcomes we can expect. Cancer stage means life and death.

Even with staging, Dr. Z said everything is going to be complicated since there were two stomach tumors together. So that could mean different treatments would be best for each of them, and different outcomes. Having two tumors also likely will limit the number of clinical trials I could be in. Clinical trials need patients with one cancer to treat, not two or three. I'm an unusual case.

"Unusual" is the last thing one wants to hear about cancer. I need a medical oncologist but not just any medical oncologist. I need the right one.

Inspiration 80

Confidence proves nothing.

Experts and the uninformed both can have complete confidence in themselves. I fancy myself a passable swordsman. Do I have any experience with a real sword? No, I have none. My ignorance gives me confidence. I don't know better. My incompetence prevents me from knowing just how awful a swordsman I am. Experts are also confident. They should be. They've earned it. When you see confidence, you don't know for sure what you are seeing. You could be facing a confident expert or a confident n00b. You have to confirm expertise.

Oddly enough, experts make a mistake only experts can make. Experts know their area so well that they forget others don't run the same rapids every day. Experts think to themselves, "Everyone knows that." Experts underestimate others' ignorance. These dual mistakes—the overconfidence of the incompetent and the overgenerosity of the expert—form the Dunning-Kruger effect. Once you see Dunning-Kruger, you can't unsee it. Dunning and Kruger are like McDonald's and Starbucks. They're everywhere.

Inspiration 79

Not thinking about something is exhausting.

Sometimes we have a thought we wish would go away. We're plagued by it. We can spend our waking hours avoiding the thought. Not thinking something is exhausting. We can't keep that up. The thought gains power the more we try not to think of it. When this happens to you, there's a way out. What can help is to let the thought take the stage of your mind. Don't fight it. Let it be there. Notice your thinking. Notice your pulse, your tension, your breath. As you do this, the thought will take its time on stage, and then it will, sooner or later, leave. Watch that too. The next time the thought comes, do the same thing. You will learn from your own experience that the thought will leave on its own.

A therapist can help you with this if it's just too much.

Schrödinger's Cancer

October 2, 2022

I had a call today from Dr. Z, my gastrointestinal oncology surgeon. Pathology took another look at my two gastric tumors. The update opens up a wider range of outcomes for me. More information means less understanding sometimes.

One gastric tumor is a diffuse adenocarcinoma of the stomach. The other is . . . well, the pathologist isn't sure. It's a gastric adenocarcinoma, the same as the other gastric cancer. But how did it get outside my stomach and to my intestine? How it got there is the problem. If the stomach tumor spread to my intestine like an oil slick, that's better, all things considered. But it's unusual. More likely is that my stomach cancer metastasized. That is, Dr. Z thinks it's more likely that my cancer has learned things we don't want cancers to learn: how to break off, float around, and make a new home in another organ.

We don't know which one happened. We won't ever know for sure. What this means, however, is that I could have stage II cancer, stage III cancer, or stage IV cancer right now. The outcomes are radically different for each of these. Stage II is mostly curable (seven in ten live). Stage III is mostly incurable (seven in ten die). Stage IV is 100% lethal. The British health system doesn't even publish five-year survival for stage IV diffuse gastric adenocarcinoma since, as they put it, "sadly most people don't live for that long after diagnosis."

I feel as if I'm Schrödinger's cat. Schrödinger's cat comes up in trivia. It's a thought experiment from quantum mechanics. Schrödinger's cat is hidden from the rest of the universe in a box along with a radioactive atom. That atom could decay and kill the cat, or the atom could remain stable and spare the cat. If we don't know which happened, Schrödinger's cat is both alive and dead at the same time. I feel physically fantastic. My future could be death in a year or survival to old age. Tumor staging is going to set the clock of my life.

I think my vision of my life would be sharp if I knew I had only a year to live. Some things would fade from my attention. Others would snap into focus as I bring my eyes close up. How do you live for tomorrow and also prepare for a long life? Different things matter.

I know we always live with many futures. Anything can happen. Usually, my future selves overlap. They blur together into one future me. Now the space between my future selves is wider than ever. I find myself choosing plans that could work for both my future selves. I guess we all do that. It's life. It's death. It's both. That dual life and death is *me* now. I can almost touch it. Whatever I do has to mean something now *and* be a worthy long-term investment. My friends and family want to exist in a reality with only one future me in mind. They want me to live. Me too. My living is the reality they choose to see. But the other reality is also mine. It's just as real.

The medium term of the next five years, where I used to live, is dead to me. I no longer have a blurred medium-future that used to be me. My future has split. I have requested work-from-home. I am turning away job recruiters who always circle. I decided to write this one book, rather than the fantasy series I always hoped to write.

My updated pathology report has two negatives that are positives. The pathologist tested two more lymph nodes for cancer. Both are negative. Also, the positive (bad) margin, which normally would have been evidence that part of my tumor had been left behind, probably isn't a bad margin after all. The pathologist agrees with Dr. Z that the bad margin is most likely in the staple line of my stomach. The stomach on the other side of the staples is free of cancer. Either another positive lymph node or a truly positive margin would have changed things for the worse.

I think the survival numbers—the statistics I have looked up in cancer journals—have to be artificially on the low side. All the five-year survival numbers are from more than five years ago with patients taking the drugs of that time. Survival statistics are the light from old stars. Treatments have improved. What are the survival numbers now? They should be higher. How much higher? I don't know. Also, averages are for the average patient. I think I must have advantages over the average patient. I live right next to Duke. I'm only fifty years old. I don't smoke or drink—never have. I have a great support system. Except for the cancer, I'm healthy. The staging numbers are probably scarier than my reality.

So much depends on my medical oncologist, who will finally stage my cancer. I meet her this week.

Inspiration 78

Every breakup is bad.

Breaking a pair bond feels awful. It seems sensible that feeling awful is our biology speaking. Mates protect each other. That's gone. Our genes have been selected to produce offspring. That's gone too. Breaking a pair bond is serious stuff, and your body knows it. The important thing to remember is this: Even the best breakup feels terrible. Feeling terrible doesn't mean you should get back together. Feeling terrible just means you broke up. Note that this is entirely theoretical biology on my part. I've never broken up with anyone. Your mother was my first and only girlfriend. And I'm A-OK with that.

Inspiration 77

Choosing feels better.

Sometimes we feel trapped. We all hate feeling trapped. It doesn't matter how nice the trap is. If we feel trapped, we hate it. It turns out we aren't really trapped as much as we may feel. We usually have options but would rather tell ourselves we have none. After all, if we are trapped, it's not our fault when things go badly. We are "trapped" in a job we hate. We are "trapped" in a marriage that isn't going the way we planned. If we choose to keep believing we have no choice, we will never fully commit. We will never be fully happy. We can't be. The way out of the trap is to choose. Start by telling yourself you are free. You quit. What do you choose now? The therapist Esther Perel put it this way: "Your first marriage is over. Would you now like to create a second one together?" You may surprise yourself by what you choose. If you choose to stay, the trap stops being a trap. Once you choose, you'll feel better about things.

Hope

October 6, 2022

I didn't realize how weighed down I've been.

For the past week I've been stuck—unsure if I had a long life or a quick death in front of me. The long life got a lot more likely this week. It feels as though much of that weight has lifted.

I met my medical oncologist and my radiation oncologist today. I like them both. They seem smart and expert in their fields. They answered all my questions. They took the time to puzzle through the staple-line complication that was confusing (even to them) in my pathology report. They admitted when they were wrong.

My medical oncologist's parents named her Hope. Hope is a good name for an oncologist, don't you think? Dr. Hope is delightfully nerdy. She loves her field. It shows. When she talks through details, she has trouble maintaining eye contact. She closes her eyes. I find it charming. She reminds me of those on the autism spectrum as they talk through their area of obsession. Before meeting Dr. Hope, I got some back-channel intelligence on her from a relative with ties to Memorial Sloan Kettering in New York. Sloan Kettering is the top cancer center on the East Coast. The Sloan Kettering doctors said Dr. Hope was the best person at Duke for gastric cancer.

We have one more piece of info from my pathology report. The pathologist found the more dangerous, more sneaky cancer in my intestine wall too. This sounds bad but is actually good. The surgeons had wondered how the visible tumor mass got to my intestine from my stomach. If the cancer metastasized from my stomach and floated to my intestine, I am in stage IV and have a year to die.

If you were my client, I would put it in a PowerPoint presentation.

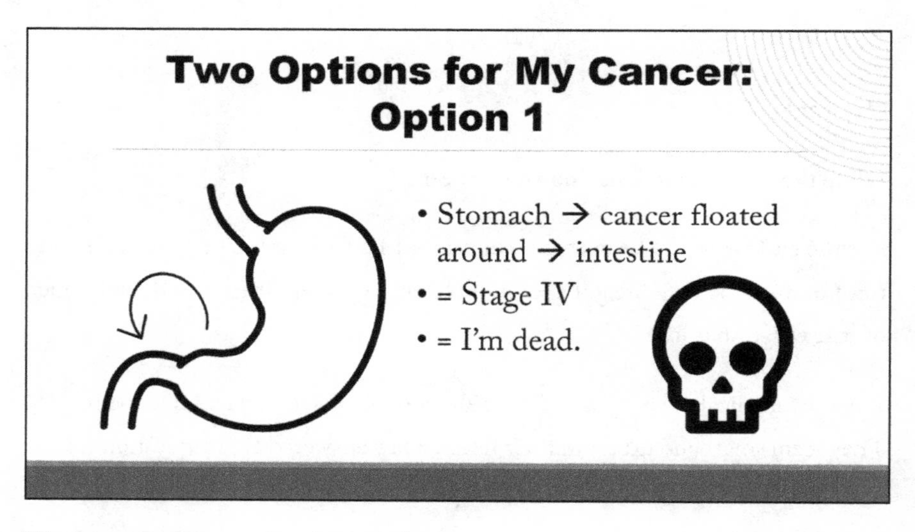

We do not recommend option number one.

The better option is option two. Option two is if the cancer moved directly from my stomach into my intestine and then mutated and burst out to make the intestinal tumor mass.

Because we now know the sneakier tumor was in the intestine also, my stomach tumor most likely spread directly to my intestine and then formed the mass. No metastasis is needed to explain what we see. The quick and bad stage IV outcome is much less likely.

**Two Options for My Cancer:
Option 2**

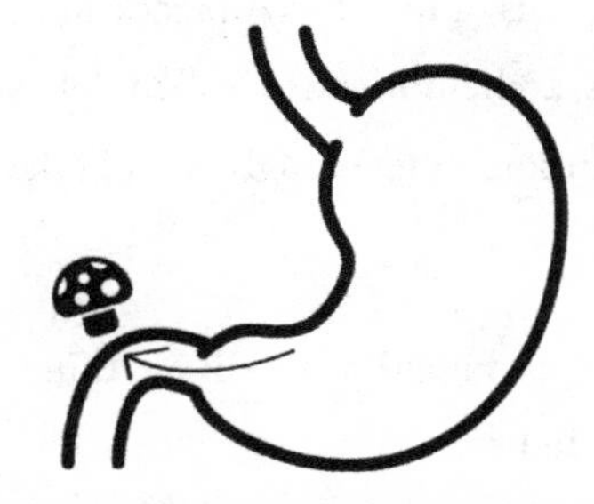

- Stomach → oozed to intestine → grew on my intestine like a mushroom
- = Stage II or III
- = I have a chance.

We recommend option number two.

Most likely my gastric tumor is stage II. That's where Dr. Hope is staging me. Stage plus treatment order gives us new survival odds. Stage II for this cancer treated by surgery first followed by chemo puts my chances of a normal lifespan somewhere between 50% and 80%. I'm pushed to the higher end by my life advantages but to the lower end because my diffuse-type gastric adenocarcinoma is more deadly. Call it two out of three. I know these numbers because Dr. Hope looked up two papers before I left the cancer center. She looked up specifically the numbers for patients who get surgery before chemo. This order of surgery first and chemo after is called adjuvant treatment. The reason I am getting adjuvant treatment is because Drs. A and Z thought I had a GIST, a different kind of intestinal tumor. Adjuvant treatment isn't recommended for my gastric cancer. The recommended course starts with chemo—which is the treatment that works better and hits cancer that has already spread—right away and is followed by surgery. Chemo-to-surgery order is called neoadjuvant therapy.

Confusing, I know. If oncology were a child's room, its floor would be strewn with Lego blocks of jargon. I keep stepping on weird words.

I start chemo on Tuesday. I will get two chemotherapies. The first chemo is intravenous oxaliplatin, which stops DNA from separating its strands when the cell tries to divide. The second chemo is an oral prodrug of 5-FU, which is a messed-up piece of DNA that starves dividing cells of new DNA pieces and hurts cells that do manage to divide. Yes, there is a chemotherapy called "eff you." Figures. My chemo has side effects but not hair loss, interestingly. I will take this chemo combo right up to the end of the year.

After that I will have a break in January and then radiation to kill anything that pops up. Nuke it from space. It's the only way to be sure.

Dr. Hope confirmed I will not be eligible for clinical trials. My kidney cancer stops that. I won't qualify. The hand I'm playing now is the hand I get.

If I survive the next couple of years without the cancer popping back up, that's when Dr. Hope said she would breathe a sigh of relief. If I survive two years after radiation, I'll probably be free.

Inspiration 76

Switch therapists if it's not working out.

The most important success factor for therapy is fit with the therapist. If you don't feel a fit, try another therapist. It doesn't make sense to tough it out. Separately, I'm sad to say that some therapists may be less interested in healing their clients than in securing recurring revenue. I've seen it. The incentives are aligned for dependency. The best way I know to protect yourself is to set a time limit for moving on. I've read that the most benefit from counseling happens in the first six months. If things are better, great. Time to move on and live your life. If things are not better, give another therapist a shot.

Inspiration 75

Name your trauma.

You may find yourself with thoughts that are so disturbing that your life becomes bent around them. You may find yourself unable to think about anything else. This could be something that happened to you. It could be something you saw. It could be something you only imagined. Everything can become a sick reminder of the one thing you don't want to think about. If this happens to you, tell someone. Tell someone about what you are thinking, all the disturbing details. You may find the thought has less hold on you. This was true of WWII Holocaust survivors. The ones who finally told their stories felt better and had to go to the hospital less. The survivors who told the most disturbing details had the most improvement. I don't know why telling someone about trauma makes things feel better. The evidence says talking helps.

Kind of a Gut Punch

October 8, 2022

Imagine finding this on your doorstep:

CAUTION

HAZARDOUS
DRUG

OBSERVE SAFETY
PRECAUTIONS FOR
HANDLING AND
ADMINISTRATION

Kind of a gut punch, isn't it?

Inspiration 74

Smart people read.

If you want to be smart, you have to read books.

Inspiration 73

You can't learn to ride a bike by reading a book.

Some things must be lived to be learned.

I Couldn't Think

Bearded son-in-law: *You got kicked out of Princeton?*

Academically, Princeton was just terrible for me. I was so excited to be in the bigs, so to speak. It was Princeton University, top ten in molecular biology, Nobel Prize in Medicine the year I joined. As I started at Princeton—and I didn't know what it was at the time—I began to have trouble focusing on classwork. I found myself not being able to learn. That's a weird feeling for someone who's always been good at learning. It's disturbing.

At the same time, I was studying for the *Jeopardy!* Tournament of Champions. I was able to keep it together for *Jeopardy!* study. *Jeopardy!* study was the one thing I could keep doing well, even when it was getting harder for me to study anything else.

We didn't really have enough money to make ends meet. I felt immense pressure to do well on the Tournament of Champions. I had expected my classwork to be easy and fun for me. It was not easy and fun for me. We were living in this tiny campus apartment with two young kids and lead paint. On top of that, the most important part of molecular biology is lab work. Lab work takes unlimited time. I didn't have unlimited time. I had no time. The stress was crushing.

I found myself going to the mall and playing video games for hours at a time. I didn't know why I was doing it. I couldn't think. I just couldn't think. I just couldn't.

Can you think of anything that might've been causing that?

It was just depression. Depression doesn't have a proximate cause. You feel like crap. There's not really a good reason. At the time, mental illness was not something that you could admit to. It's not how it is now.

Not like what it is now, where "you got to get help."

Even to get to see a medical doctor, I had to go through counseling gatekeepers. I told the counselor, "I don't think I need to talk to you. I think something's wrong in my brain. I don't know what it is, but it is not right. I need medicine."

I flew back to California to play in the $100,000 *Jeopardy!* Tournament of Champions. That much money would have financed grad school. The competitors were scary good. Some were every bit as fast on the buzzer as I was. Two players were faster. Most knew more than I did. I scraped by in the first round with a good but not great score. In the second round, I got lottery-ticket lucky. The best player—the one we other contestants whispered about in the green room—forgot the category in Final Jeopardy. Forgot the category. That doesn't happen. Nobody on *Jeopardy!* is going to forget the Final Jeopardy category was "Democrats" and write down "Lincoln," the most famous Republican. That certainly doesn't happen on the Tournament of Champions. It definitely doesn't happen to the best player in the tournament. But that's what happened. He was leading. I could barely catch him by betting it all. His mistake put me into the finals.

I was the fastest player in the finals. I led both days going into Final Jeopardy. I bet it all both days. I got one of the two Final Jeopardy clues right. I got the other one wrong. I lost by a single dollar. I lost to the first woman to win the *Jeopardy!* Tournament of Champions. I was happy for her. It was about time that a woman won the Tournament of Champions. I think feeling honestly happy for her helped me be okay with my just missing winning. Winning would have paid $100,000. I got second place and another $20,800. That second-place purse helped.

After *Jeopardy!* I was recognized everywhere. "Are you Jeff?" I got asked that on public transport in London, New York, and Amsterdam. Passengers called out my name as I boarded airplanes. I got asked for autographs. It's odd to be on display. It's odd to walk down the street and have people stare. Fame is kind of fun. Fame is kind of creepy. A young woman stopped me in the mall. She stared right at me without blinking, said my wife hadn't seemed all that loving on *Jeopardy!* and asked if we were having marital problems. Yeah—a little creepy.

Back at the Princeton health center, the counselors finally decided I was depressed enough for them and referred me to a medical doctor. The doctor was dismissive but put me on Prozac anyway. Prozac is not a great drug, but it helped. It helped take the edge off a little bit. By that point I was not doing at all well in classes.

As well as *Jeopardy!* had gone, school was going poorly. Princeton asked me to leave. They told me it wasn't working out. Even with the *Jeopardy!* money, I couldn't afford to leave. I needed the crappy stipend. I needed the married student housing for my family. I told the program chair what had been going on with my depression. He let me know they weren't happy but the program would give me a bit of reprieve. I needed to start doing better fast and to spend more time in the lab.

Grad school in science expects you to work long hours and do what you're told. You're cheap manual labor. I didn't know at first I was cheap manual labor. But that's what I was. I started to figure out how the world works. I went more often to the lab. I performed my assigned tasks. But I never found my place. Slime molds were pretty but not for me. Bacteria lab: no. The cancer lab of the Famous

Man was toxic—famously so, as came out later in national news. Finally, I landed in a mouse biology lab. It wasn't right for me. None of the labs were right for me. Working at the bench wasn't right for me.

It turns out I'm not good in a molecular biology lab. I'm not careful enough, not even close to it. Lab work is precise work. I'm not precise. This is funny because I can cook you a meal you'd remember in a good way. Try to get me to get molecular biology experiments to work . . . not a good idea.

I tried to stick it out my second year. The Prozac wasn't enough. I was still depressed. It was better than it had been, but it wasn't enough. As I would walk to school, I would have pictures of destruction, explosions running through my head. I wasn't suicidal, but I didn't want to live. When I lived in the West, I always knew where I was. The mountains were always there like a wall my eyes could rest against. You find true north without needing a street sign. At Princeton, there are no mountains. There is no distant horizon. The green and the houses close in around you. I noticed it. I noticed it every day. I felt closed in, trapped. I would drive and never know which direction was what.

No matter how awful I felt, I was determined to show them. I was just going to do it. I went up for my oral exams. I failed. That's it. You're out of here. I was mortified.

I wish I knew why a professor named Martin did what he did for me. He had an immunology lab, and he was a name in molecular biology. While I was there, he got inducted into the National Academy of Sciences. He discovered one of the three "stop" codons—three-letter DNA codes that tell your body to stop adding amino acids to a protein. That was a big deal. His lab worked on lupus, an autoimmune disease where the immune system, mostly in women, attacks the body's own DNA. For whatever reason, Martin made me his lab technician. I was still kicked out of Princeton. I was no longer a student. But as a lab tech, I could take classes. I could do research. I could keep my hopes alive of getting back in the molecular biology program—the program I had wanted to love, the program I had wanted to love me.

Inspiration 72

Depression is more than “really sad.”

If you haven’t been depressed, thank the god of your choice. You may think you know what depression is. You don’t. There was nothing in my experience that prepared me for depression. Depression is not just sadness. If sadness is a dark night, depression is a cave: You see nothing. What works for sadness may do nothing for depression. Trust me. I tried. Depression doesn’t mean you are lazy. Depression doesn’t mean you are weak. Don’t beat yourself up over being depressed and unable to will your way out of it. If you are depressed, seek professional help. Your depression may need medical treatment. As you understand your depression, you may find it visits for a day or a week and then leaves for a time. Knowing depression has its season and is not forever can help. Wait it out. Many of us grow out of depression over time. I did. Mostly.

Inspiration 71

You'll feel better in the morning.

When you are filled with despair, get some sleep. I'm not saying you'll feel *all* better in the morning. But you will feel better.

So That's What Chemo Is Like

October 11, 2022

So that's what chemo is like. It's not fun. But it's also not give-me-weed-now bad.

The chemo at Duke is pumped into patients in what feels like a cross between an exam room and a nursing home. The door is a curtain. Each room is built around an infusion chair. Think dentist chair plus La-Z-Boy. Charming. You can recline without it being comfortable.

The nursing staff was kind and careful. My nurse confirmed that I was actually me and that I indeed wanted to get the chemotherapy oxaliplatin. I guess, yes? She got the IV started. The chemotherapy was clear. I was thankful for that. Some chemo is red and nicknamed the "red devil." I know color doesn't matter, but somehow it did.

That's where I sat for the next five hours.

The side effects introduced themselves in minutes. My ginger ale decided to punch me in my salivary glands. It tasted awful—like lime juice concentrate. The ginger ale was so sour my salivary glands ached. The worse side effect kicked in after about two hours. My infusion arm began to burn. There wasn't a pool of fluid under my skin that would have meant my vein was blown. But it hurt. That's a possible side effect of oxaliplatin. It felt as if my arm were on fire at the same time that the nurse's light touch felt soothing—both at once, which is an impossible feeling. The burning was also like electric shocks or pins and needles, but nothing really captures it. The burning stopped at a clear line on my forearm. When I got home, I marked out the border with a Sharpie pen. The marker traced a shape from my left wrist to the inside of my elbow in, I noticed, a near-perfect map of Madagascar.

The nurse called in a backup for a second opinion. The attending physician drifted by to offer a third opinion. "Does the vein look blown to you?" They couldn't decide. They switched arms and got the rest of the chemo in me. That arm started burning too.

When I got home, I started in on the oral chemo.

Dr. Hope warned me that peak side effects would be day three post-infusion. That's this Friday. I have an important client meeting on Friday. I can't move it.

Inspiration 70

Grade the test to ace the test.

Seek out opportunities to be a judge. Grade papers. Interview job applicants. Help pick a vendor. There is no better way to learn how a judge thinks than to be one. After being a judge, you'll find it's a lot easier to impress the next one.

Inspiration 69

Let your joy win and your craving lose.

Craving is one feeling. Enjoyment is another. The two feelings are different. I crave a Reuben sandwich. I crave one right now. But every time I bite into a Reuben, I feel sick. There is something about the oil, salt, and sour that sound so good but make me want to barf as soon as I bite. Notice how much joy you get. Pay special attention when your craving and enjoyment don't match. Avoid things that you crave but that you don't actually enjoy. Consciously choose things you enjoy that you don't naturally crave. When we pay attention to what gives us joy, we make better choices. I've had to learn to ignore my craving for a Reuben. I remember it's never as good as my craving tells me. I remember my past nausea. I happily order a different sandwich. Usually.

I Didn't Feel Great

October 17, 2022

The next day I didn't feel . . . great. I had cleared my main client presentations through the end of the week. Unfortunately, I had to get a lot of work done. I was up working until 4:00 A.M. for a Friday client meeting I couldn't move. Big client. Big project. Don't judge.

By Thursday, my guts felt a little off. Lots of rumbling. Hmm. The chemo was carpet-bombing my gut bacteria and killing off the lining of my intestines. They had started to leak.

I felt dehydrated. The muscles in my eye sockets cramped when I yawned. I felt sunken in. I switched from water to Gatorade, which is what they give cholera patients so they don't defecate themselves to death.

If the Gatorade had helped, I don't want to know what sticking with tap water would have done. On Friday I had to cut that big client meeting short. I tried to go the distance. So started three days of diarrhea. When I wasn't on the toilet, I felt that I'd be wiser being on the toilet anyway. I compromised and put some towels down on the bed.

I didn't end up needing the towels. Simple pleasures are the best.

I was also having the weird cold sensitivity the nurse had warned me about. Touching cold things for a few seconds caused the same burning pain I had felt in my forearms. I tried to chew my beloved ice from my beloved home ice machine ("the good ice"). No dice. It felt as if I got the burn and bite of Diet Coke carbonation on my tongue, minus the Diet Coke. Add a touch of Taser.

I also started getting chills. Normally, I like the fan on when I sleep. Not now. I bought an electric blanket. I'm using it at night and sometimes during work meetings when I can turn off my camera.

I sent Dr. Hope pictures of my Sharpied arms. She ordered a chemo port for me so the arm-burning side effect doesn't happen again. A port is a reservoir that will be surgically implanted under the skin of my chest. The port will be my new chemo vein. Chemo will be injected into my port, and from there the port will carry the chemo through my jugular vein into my heart's right atrium, which is too large to leak the way my arm veins did.

Port-installation surgery is in three days.

Inspiration 68

Your commute will crush your soul.

You will never get those hours back. A short commute is worth more than you think.

Inspiration 67

Distance can pry a family apart.

Families do better together. Working far from family is hard on everyone. Working even six weeks away from you kids and your mother eroded my mental health. I could feel it. Even a healthy marriage has gaps that can be pried apart as if by a knife tip in shellfish. I don't think my working in different states from you my first year as a consultant helped any of you kids either. Sometimes distance work is the job. The military, transportation, and foreign service separate families. Working apart from family may be your best choice but don't decide that on autopilot. Place a high value on working where you can live together.

The Last Thing I Remember

October 22, 2022

This week I felt progressively better. We got the client project done and delivered Friday at 10:00 P.M. I promised it would be delivered Friday. We delivered Friday. It's not always like this, but sometimes it is.

I felt well enough to start walking the greenway again. I just tested, and my cold sensitivity is gone. I'm back on Diet Coke and the good ice. I no longer need my electric blanket.

I had the port-installation surgery. Even though I've now driven to the cancer center at least ten times, I kept making wrong turns on the way. I was thinking through a math problem from work, which messes up my ability to navigate. But I also think I must have been scared of the surgery without realizing it.

It took multiple needle sticks for the nurses to get my sedation IV started. I guess I won't need needle sticks again with the port.

I have no memory post-sedation. What I do remember is the physician's assistant. He was a talker. I asked about the X-ray source hanging above me. He was game to answer. As he satisfied my curiosity about X-rays, he shaved my chest hair over the port implantation site with a pair of electric clippers. The clippers were dull, so he tossed them in the trash and got some sharp ones. The nurse was pretty uptight about tossing the dull electric clippers in the trashcan rather than the medical sharps disposal for used syringes and scalpels. The assistant rolled his eyes, fished the dull clippers from the regular trash, relegated said clippers to the sharps disposal, and proceeded to ask anyone who wandered into our suite if dull electric clippers should be thrown in the regular trash or in the sharps disposal. (Regular trash.) He was relentless. When he was done shaving—between quizzing passersby about proper dull-clipper disposal—he strapped me down on the surgical bed. He noted the bed was narrow and that the strap would keep me from falling. It sounded to me that there must be a story there. Hospital safety measures often come with stories. So I asked the assistant if anyone ever fell. He paused for a second—maybe thinking of the way sedation can mess with memory. Then he told me all about the time he walked into a surgical suite to find a 350-pound woman on the floor. He had to muster all hands on deck to get the woman back on the surgical bed. The nurse at the time was apparently crying about possibly losing her job.

That's the last thing I remember from port surgery.

The port hurts. I think it should be better next week. With the port, they will be able to draw blood and to infuse chemo without it scorching my arms. My left arm still burns from the chemo. Hopefully that's not permanent.

My port looks as if it's from the first frame of a cyst-removal video. The port is hard. It feels as though half a golf ball is under the skin of my right pec. The incision is longer than any of the ones used to remove my tumors. I have a second incision under my collarbone. A tube worms up from the port to the second incision. That tube is threaded through my jugular vein right into my heart. And that's my port.

I'm still waiting for my next-generation genetic sequencing so we know what next-generation drugs my cancer might respond to if things go badly.

Inspiration 66

Be a friend to anyone. Choose wisely whom you follow.

Most parents will tell you to choose your friends carefully. I won't. Be a friend to anyone. What I will counsel you is to choose carefully whom you follow. Choose whom you admire, will be influenced by, imitate. If you choose the wrong people to follow, you may sink with them. Even when you find someone worth being followed, everyone makes mistakes. Never follow any person fully.

Inspiration 65

They'll grow into the goodness you name.

Some people just need their goodness to be noticed and named. Name it, and they will live up to it. Name their best parts. "You're the kind of person who . . ." inspires others to live up to what you see in them.

Little Sputniks

October 25, 2022

I got another test result back. This one is for microsatellite instability. I had to look that up.

> Mismatch repair: INTACT
>
> Immunohistochemistry: Normal result.
>
> Expression of MLH1, MSH2, MSH6, and PMS2 is retained in the neoplastic cells.
>
> PCR: Microsatellite stable (MSS).

When a protein that normally fixes broken DNA gets broken, that can cause cancer. Four of those repair proteins are MLH1, MSH2, MSH6, and PMS2. These proteins repair DNA mismatches. Mismatch-repair proteins fix DNA when one of the two strands has the wrong code.

What this result tells me is that my mismatch repair is working. The mismatch-repair proteins look normal. That's the immunohistochemistry part. The other way we know my mismatch repair is fine is microsatellite stability. When mismatch repair is working, small repeated pieces of DNA act the way they should. These small DNA repeats are called microsatellites. Microsatellites are not little Sputniks. When mismatch repair is broken, different cancer cells have different numbers of DNA microsatellites. When the lab looked at my microsatellites, my cancer cells had the same number of microsatellite copies from cell to cell. My microsatellites are stable. So my mismatch repair is intact.

This means two things for me, one good and one meh.

Good thing: I don't have Lynch syndrome. Lynch syndrome is a genetic disease with broken mismatch repair. Lynch syndrome would have meant more cancers for me. We can rule that out. We also don't have to worry about my kids having Lynch syndrome.

The meh thing: If I had had messed-up mismatch-repair genes, immunotherapies called PD-1 inhibitors could have been useful in treating me. Since I don't have messed-up mismatch repair, PD-1 inhibitors aren't yet called for. Mismatch-repair screw-ups aren't the only reason to take PD-1 inhibitors, so they aren't completely off the table.

What I still haven't seen is my full genetic profile, so-called next-generation sequencing. I want that since it will provide a fuller list of what chemotherapies I could take in the future. Knowing the details in advance matters. I've been waiting on this. The next-generation sequencing was not ordered despite both surgeons saying it was standard. I think the surgeons were thinking about the microsatellite instability test. Dr. Hope said she would order the next-generation sequencing.

Dr. Hope reminded me that whatever sequencing tells us will be useful only if my cancer progresses. Progression is not a good thing. Progression means spread. Then, we'd be looking at a fatal outcome in less than a year, and the newer drugs would give me additional months of life.

That's why I'm pushing to have the testing done now. If we need to select the right drug, there will be no time to waste.

Inspiration 64

Pay off credit cards.

There is no day your mom and I felt more financial relief than when we finally paid off our credit cards. During grad school, we built up a credit-card balance trying to kick our way to the surface. You know that feeling of being watched? When we paid off those credit cards, I realized I had been feeling as though I were being watched. I had been feeling as though I were being watched by some predator. I had felt that every day. When we paid off those credit cards, I finally felt as if I didn't have to hide.

Inspiration 63

Invest simply. Avoid fees.

Invest in an index fund with the lowest management fees. That's long been a Vanguard fund. I chose Vanguard's S&P 500 tracking fund. Max out employer investment-matching. Don't waste your time picking stocks unless you do it for a living. *Really* don't pay other people to gamble with your money. That's what hiring a fund manager amounts to. Should you pick stocks yourself? No. The index funds are less work and less risk. Active trading is just another way of saying "casino." I say this as someone who was trained to pick stocks in business school and ran some endowment funds. I doubled Notre Dame's money in six months. I was good at it. Trust me on this. The way to win the stock-picking game is to diversify with an index fund and avoid fees.

Ever Seen *Pulp Fiction?*

October 31, 2022

Happy Halloween. Today was my second chemo infusion.

My chemo port is an improvement over IVs. No more getting the IV sticks or blood draws. No more burning arm pain. I will say it's alarming to get the needle stick in the port the first time. It's not a gentle "little sting, Mr. Stewart." It's more like "let's stab you in the chest." Ever seen *Pulp Fiction?*

It was over quickly but *ouch*. I'm totally going to be a baby and pick up the anesthetic lidocaine gel from the pharmacy next time.

I brought my first oral chemo pills with me to the infusion center. I didn't know if I should take the first ones right away or in the evening. I carried the chemo pills loose in my jeans pocket. My infusion nurse watched me fish the pills out of my jeans. She froze. It was as though I had just pulled a live coral snake from my pocket.

"Mr. Stewart, when you take those pills, you shouldn't touch them. You should pour the pills carefully in the medicine bottle cap, swallow them, then wash your hands." Oh. I gather I shouldn't be leaving a residue of mutagenic, messed-up pieces of DNA around. Good to know.

November 2, 2022

My care team warned that my side effects would get worse each infusion. They were right about that.

I don't know what it feels like to play with a vat of electric eels, but I imagine it's what I'm feeling when I wash my hands. Everything cold zaps.

I'm low on potassium. The potato soup I'm supposed to be eating to raise my potassium levels is in the cold fridge. That's kind of a problem. I can touch the lid only through my jacket. My hands are zappy much of the time. I even had to wear ski gloves to the pizzeria.

I'm not actually cold. No chills.

Inspiration 62

You can choose to seethe over others' success or warm yourself over it.

Other people will get the success you want. You may want that success so much it burns. You may want their money. You may want their job. You may want their life. Some childhood friends will achieve the success you always thought would be yours and never theirs. Your choice will be how you live with their success. You can choose to live with their success badly. You can choose to seethe. Or you can choose to make peace with their success. Good for them! The more you delight in the success of others, the happier you'll be. Their success probably didn't hurt you. Their success may even be a road map you can use. It'll be hard to hold that road map if you're raising your fists to the sky.

Inspiration 61

Sometimes we just need to hold the light.

Sometimes we find friends in despair. They've lost something. They've lost someone. They see no way out. If we can help, we help. But if we can't help, we can still hold the light. Sometimes we just need to hold the light for them for a while. Listen to them. Hear their pain. Name it. Be there. Don't try to solve what you can't. Don't try to explain their pain away. Just hold the light. Sometimes that's what they need.

Yeah, I Cried

Bearded son-in-law: *You were a lab tech but not a Princeton student anymore?*

I was indignant that the school refused to see my value. Surely, they just needed more time. So I stayed, and I stayed. They wanted me to go. They were angry at me for staying. I was a thorn in their side. I was also kind of famous from *Jeopardy!* so it was all kinds of bad.

We had to move out of student housing. My technician pay wouldn't cover rent in Princeton. I was a lab tech, not a student, so we couldn't take out more student loans. We moved in with Jen's parents. I started commuting an hour each way. Sometimes I would sleep in the lab.

My advisor, Martin, didn't have me work at the experimentation bench. He had me work on theory. That was different. When I said Princeton was a bad place for me, it was because Princeton was as experimental a molecular biology program as you could find. With Martin, I found myself doing something I love. I love theory. Every day I would analyze virus sequences, run immune system simulations, or figure out new things from antibody DNA. I put math and biology together. I worked on a computer.

I remember sitting in front of the computer and thinking, "This is work. I am working. I am sitting here in front of a computer working." That was a new feeling for a guy from The Dalles, Oregon, who was used to judging people by looking at their hands and seeing if they had embedded dirt—a real worker.

Big, meaty hands.

That's right. Big, meaty hands.

I found myself having intellectual conversations with delightful people, especially two visiting researchers: a physicist named Phil and a statistician named Sam. Huh. Phil the Physicist and Sam the Statistician. I didn't realize that until right now. Funny. With Phil and Sam, I published my first paper, "A Solution to the Rheumatoid Factor Paradox." Phil died of cancer years ago. We published our last paper together after he died. Sam's in his nineties now. He's a working statistician at Fox Chase Cancer Center. He's still sharp. I send him science fiction recommendations, and he sends me math puzzles. Sam, his wife, and I have a patent together on how to analyze viral quasispecies.

As I started publishing papers with Phil the Physicist and Sam the Statistician, I tried to get Princeton to let me back into the PhD program. They kept saying *no* each year. If I had had a lick of sense, I would've just moved on. I already had good contacts with a coauthor at Yale. But by that point I was invested in never giving up. There's no wall I would not fight through, or so I thought. I loved the work. By that time, I'd published more papers than any of my classmates. Didn't matter.

One day the strangest thing happened. It was like nothing I've felt before or since. I was walking down the lab hallway, and it was as if a laser cut straight through the top of my head. It just beamed an idea into my head. I knew then and there why women get autoimmune disease. It was so clear to me. Women get autoimmune disease far more often than men, sometimes ten times as often.

Wow. Why?

People said hormones. This is not a satisfying answer because it's not as if changing hormones cures autoimmunity. It doesn't. Hormone levels don't correlate with autoimmunity either. "It's hormones" is kind of a lame answer, to be honest. It could be true, but it didn't seem to be predictive, and it didn't seem to be right. When I was there, walking down that hallway, everything snapped into place. A bunch of things I had been studying all clicked together.

I'll take two minutes to explain what the heck's going on—or at least what I think is going on. Your immune system has to tell what's you and what's not you. If it's you, no attack. If it's not you, attack. This is called self/nonself recognition. It's the core of immunology. What I realized in the lab hallway was that women aren't like men to an immune system. That's because men have only one X chromosome. Women have two. Women don't keep both their X chromosomes on all the time. Instead, each female cell has one X chromosome turned on and the other one turned off, permanently. This means that there isn't one self when it comes to women. Women have two selves, one for each X chromosome. We can see these two different selves in calico cats. A calico's color patterns are made by the two X chromosomes. That's why calico cats are female or the rare XXY male. Women have stripes, believe it or not. Women look like tigers at the molecular level. The stripes are called Blaschko's lines. We don't normally see Blaschko's lines because human skin color genes aren't on the X chromosome the way they are on calico cats. But autoimmune attacks can run along the stripes that are there under the surface. That's another clue. I realized that if the conditions were just right, these X-chromosome patterns would cause a woman's immune system to think part of her body was an infectious disease. Women's X chromosomes could cause autoimmunity.

I spent about six months reading everything I could find about the immune system and X chromosomes. I wrote up my theory for publication. I had no coauthors. It was just me. A high-circulation immunology journal accepted my paper. When I cracked open the box with my twenty author copies, I saw what I hadn't even hoped to expect. My paper was on the cover of *Immunology Today*. The cover was made up to look like the television show *The X-Files*. That was a big, big moment for me. ABC radio in Australia picked it up in their "great moments of science" series. They didn't know that Jeffrey Stewart of Princeton University was Jeffrey Stewart, the lab tech the university couldn't stand.

I'm surprised you don't have that magazine cover on the wall.

I thought about putting it up in here for Zoom meetings. It's in the bookshelf somewhere.

Little trophy.

It was fun, especially given the background of such, to me, disturbing experiences. Those experiences, on the bright side, gave me compassion for people who don't do as well in school. I've been there.

Even if they did let you do your thing, of course, they're going to make it like hell for you. They might let you win, but they're going to try their best to throw you off.

They did, yes.

Do you want to live with that stress? You had enough going on with the depression and the living situation. And at that point you had three kids?

Four. We had Jessica, also, and Aidan was born right at the end of Princeton.

Lot of stress.

And just, you know, not enough money and trying to make ends meet. It was very, very hard.

I did finally decide after three years of trying that Princeton was never going to let me back into its PhD program. The university awarded me my master's degree, which is kind of a booby prize in molecular biology. I left and went to do theoretical biology at Los Alamos National Laboratory, where they invented the atomic bomb.

It took another seven years for experimentalists in Turkey and the Netherlands to confirm the predictions my autoimmunity theory made. X chromosomes aren't the only reason women get autoimmune disease, but it looks as if it's one of the reasons. My key prediction was that immune system X chromosomes would have a highly skewed pattern in autoimmune women. These women would have almost all their immune system cells with the same X chromosome on. No balance. That's exactly what the experimentalists found. In three autoimmune diseases, X chromosomes are highly skewed. The best proof came from a natural experiment of identical twin sisters. Identical twin sisters share the same DNA but not the same X-chromosome patterns. In sisters where one twin had autoimmune thyroiditis and the other didn't, the healthy twin had balanced X-chromosome patterns. But the identical twin, the one with autoimmune disease, had high X-chromosome skew. It was a perfect match to what my theory predicted. When I saw that, yeah, I cried.

Inspiration 60

Failure is the tuition we pay to learn compassion.

We pay to learn compassion. The price we pay is failure. Failure carves on our headstone "I understand. I've been there."

Inspiration 59

When it's hopeless, you're the hope.

I adore Mr. Rogers. "When I was a boy," he said, "and I would see scary things in the news, my mother would say to me, 'Look for the helpers. You will always find people who are helping.'" I don't think Mr. Rogers said this only to comfort scared children. Read between his lines. He was calling us to action. He was asking us to do more. Don't just look for the helpers. Be a helper. When things fall apart, be the one who puts things right. Be the answer to another's prayer. Why shouldn't it be you?

Seven Percent

November 4, 2022

Cancer patients who choose alternative therapy over mainstream medicine double their risk of death.

As a cancer patient, I'm getting forwarded many, many articles about early stage cancer treatments and alternative therapies. I think every cancer patient gets these. I'm public about my cancer, so I'm getting these from more than friends and family. I'm getting these also from people I've never met but who are trying to help.

Cancer treatments are not just a personal interest. Part of my job for over fifteen years has been to advise pharma companies on cancer drugs. My clients have included big pharma and small biotechs. You'd know the big-pharma names. I've interviewed hundreds of oncologists over the years. Figuring out the scientific and commercial potential of a cancer drug is a normal day on the job for me.

Basic rule of cancer treatments: Evidence wins. We need evidence to believe anything works. That's especially true for cancer.

Step one: Is the drug FDA-approved?

Step two: If the drug is approved, is the drug also recommended in cancer guidelines? If the approved drug is not in cancer guidelines, insurance companies aren't going to pay.

Step three: If the drug is neither approved nor in guidelines, is the drug in late-stage clinical trials? That usually means phase III. If so, then maybe a cancer patient can join those. If not in late-stage clinical trials, the drug is too early in testing to help most people who have cancer now.

Amazing result in a test tube? Talk to me in fifteen years if I'm still here. Just started phase I clinical trials in people? Still too early to help me. Cures mice? Of all the oncologists I've interviewed about mouse data, I've been told by at least a quarter of them this exact punchline: "I've never treated a mouse for cancer." Yuk, yuk. Funny oncologists. It's not just snark. They have a point buried under their tired joke. Most things that cure cancer in mice don't work in people. It's worse than you imagine.

Nearly every new thing coming out of a university is too early to help anyone who has cancer now. Worse, nearly everything fails. If that sounds jaded, I'm sorry. This is oncologists' lived reality. Yes, there have been great strides in cancer treatment. The really promising drugs that can do anything in the short term are already in late-stage clinical trials. Oncologists read. They know what's coming. Anything early stage will not, cannot cure someone who has cancer now. I have to think one of the worst parts of an oncologist's job is to explain why a miracle cure in early development holds no promise at all for a cancer patient today.

Here's what most people not immersed in oncology don't get. Even the most promising cancer drugs fail. Cancer drugs have the second-worst failure rate of any disease. Only Alzheimer's is worse. Think of the tens of millions of dollars spent to get one cancer drug out of a university, into cell lines and mice, and finally into patients to be tested in clinical trials. That's a huge effort. It might take a decade. Those drugs that get tested in people have won a biotech lottery. For any cancer drug to be tested in people, the science has to be *amazing*. Scientists working on the drug believe it's a lock to work. There may be talk of a Nobel Prize or at least the Lasker Award. Everything seems sure to succeed. What could go wrong?

Do you want to take a guess at how many of those "sure winners" end up passing clinical trials? Seven percent. That's 7% of the best drugs that emerged from the best science and were so promising that a pharma company invested $10 million to more than $1 billion to test the drugs in patients. Ninety-three percent of the "winners" fail.

What about repurposed approved drugs? Approved drugs can be used off label by physicians. What if, say, an anti-parasite drug cured cancer? Why not take that?

The question is, again, where is the evidence? Cancer drugs are special. State laws require insurance companies to pay for cancer drugs any time independent cancer guidelines say the drugs should be used. Even if the drug is not FDA-indicated for the cancer, so long as the evidence shows the drug works, insurance companies must pay. Leading oncologists update cancer guidelines whenever the evidence gets good enough.

You see where this is going? For an approved drug not to be on cancer guidelines, the evidence sucks.

This is what I do when I'm forwarded information about nonstandard, alternative, or early cancer therapies: I hit delete. I know, even without reading, the evidence isn't there yet. Things that look fantastic almost always fail. Anything early stage is not helpful for anyone who has cancer now.

Snake-oil sellers are all over cancer patients. They are all over me. These hucksters will make a buck ripping off cancer patients if they can. These hucksters are vultures (or optimistic to the point of delusion). They don't have evidence. See above.

Even legitimate innovators have a hard time imagining it's possible their cancer drug will fail. But their cancer drug will fail most of the time. It's not something scientists like to admit to themselves.

If you want to take an unproven libido booster, that's one thing. But cancer? Don't waste the time you have left.

What is a cancer patient supposed to do when the standard treatments seem to be pointless? What if the odds with standard treatments are so bad that there might as well be no treatment at all? I'd say to ask your oncologist if there are promising, late-stage clinical trials you can join. This is a perfect question. A late-stage clinical trial is the best chance a cancer patient has to get a next-generation treatment before approval. We're in a golden age of cancer immunotherapy. There are promising immunotherapies in late-stage clinical trials. If you're enrolled in a trial, not only do you get a chance for a new treatment, you will help move the science along so future patients may benefit. You may even get paid. This is exactly what I tried to do for myself. I don't qualify because I have two different kinds of tumors, but I'm an unusual case.

Inspiration 58

Hoard your decisions. You have only a few good ones to spend each day.

Our decision-making capacity is finite. We have only so many good decisions in us each day. Every decision is a withdrawal from our mental reserves. I wear black polo shirts every day because I don't want to spend decisions on my wardrobe. When we deplete the mental energy we have, we start making bad decisions. We develop decision fatigue.

Once we understand good decisions are a finite resource, we can have more compassion for the poor. Big decisions make big withdrawals from our daily decision bank. Think about your day. Think about all the decisions you made. Now think about your same day but with only $25 to spend. How many gallons of gas can you pump? Which would you rather have shut off, the water or the heat? Are you sure you want fries with that? The poor must make big decisions every day. You probably didn't have to think twice.

Inspiration 57

Not choosing is the worst choice.

We never have just two choices. We always have at least three. We can choose A. We can choose B. We can also choose not to make a choice. Our time runs out, and we are stuck with something that happens to us, not something we chose to choose. The worst choice is often not choosing.

What if it's a hard choice? When we have a hard choice to make, it's actually an easy choice. A hard choice is hard because we can't tell which choice is better. It's too close to call. Whatever we choose will probably be fine. The only hard part about a hard choice is choosing to choose. Just do it. Flip a coin if that helps. If you regret seeing tails, flip again until you get heads.

Not Good

November 9, 2022

My next-generation sequencing is back.

> Tumor Mutational Burden - 2 Muts/Mb No therapies or clinical trials.
>
> FGFR2 amplification, 10 Trials, Futibatinib, Pazopanib.
>
> Disease relevant genes with no reportable alterations: ERBB2.

This report was generated after the hospital sent my tumor off to have its DNA analyzed. Depending on the mutations, Dr. Hope could have more tools to put in her utility belt. There was lot to unpack. I had to look up some papers to understand it all. I'm waiting on Dr. Hope to confirm. Here's what the report means to me.

There is one good thing in the report. I don't have a known genetic condition that causes cancer. The mutation we see was made by my cancer. It's not baked into the rest of my DNA. I didn't put my kids at risk by being their dad.

I have a deadly mutation of a gene called fibroblast growth factor receptor 2, or *FGFR2*. In my gastric tumor, the *FGFR2* gene is amplified, which means my cancer made Xerox copies of the DNA for this gene. More *FGFR2* helps cancer be cancer.

The worst part about the genetic profile is how quickly I could die. I tracked down studies on the survival times for those with the *FGFR2* amplification in my kind of cancer. For my stage or worse, the survival time was five months. That sounds scarier than it is. The number is misleading since it includes patients with later-stage cancer in the mix. There was a lot of stage IV cancer in there. My cancer is stage IIa. The important part for me is that patients with *FGFR2*-amplified cancers die about nine months sooner. If my cancer progresses, we already knew I was going to die from it. What we now know is that the end will probably come quickly if my cancer spreads.

What we can't tell from the published papers is if the overall odds of my cancer spreading are worse because of *FGFR2*. Probably the odds are worse, but here I'm speculating. Informed guess: We're back to a coin flip.

Targeting the FGFR2 protein is probably a good idea. There are two cancer drugs that may work against FGFR2. Two more drugs to treat my tumors is good news. It's just not good news for me. Neither drug is approved for my kind of cancer. So that's out. I checked, and the drugs do not appear yet in oncology guidelines for my cancer. These guidelines are oncology cookbooks. Not being in guidelines means the evidence isn't in. Even if my cancer worsens and even though there is reason to believe the drugs would help me, my insurance company may not let me try these drugs off label.

There are ten clinical trials targeting the FGFR2 protein with these two drugs. That would normally mean I would think about joining these trials. I won't qualify, however, because I had the kidney tumor too. No clinical trials for me.

The rest of the genetic profile tells me that I can't use other targeted therapies. I had hoped for *ERBB2* to tell the oncologists I should use a targeted cancer agent called Herceptin. I remember reading *Her2: The Making of Herceptin* my last year at Princeton. Herceptin revolutionized breast cancer treatment. But, no, my tumor doesn't look as if it will be helped by Herceptin. I had also hoped a reason to take PD-1 inhibitors would be found in my genes. PD-1 inhibitors are new, potent immunotherapies. No dice. As we already knew, the microsatellite instability said PD-1 inhibitors weren't likely to be helpful. That's confirmed. Also, my cancer has a low mutational burden of two mutations per million DNA base pairs. A low mutational burden is another sign that PD-1 inhibitors won't work for my tumors. Darn.

Bottom line: The next-generation sequencing does not change my treatment. If my cancer does spread, my death will more likely be rapid. It's hard to imagine that a cancer that kills more quickly doesn't spread more easily. I think it's also more likely my *FGFR2*-amplified cancer will spread.

I'll write quickly.

Inspiration 56

Truth first.

If it's not true, don't believe it. Don't say it. Don't live it. It doesn't matter if everyone else believes a lie. Take one step down that ravine, and there is no depth to which you may not tumble.

Inspiration 55

If it helps people, I'm for it. If it hurts people, I'm against it.

How do we know what will hurt or help? We don't need to solve advanced moral calculus. I think we just know. Our conscience tells us. I reflect often on the advice a parish priest gave to a young John Rock. Rock was the co-inventor of the birth control pill. "John, always stick to your conscience. Never let anyone else keep it for you. And I mean anyone else." Dr. Rock had seen the suffering of his patients—Boston mothers who endured multiple miscarriages, mothers who couldn't care for the children they had. John Rock's patients needed birth control. He knew how to help. But Rock was Roman Catholic. Birth control was forbidden. Rock followed his conscience. He successfully lobbied (hard) to have the FDA approve the pill. Rock was ostracized for it. His kids were too. Even the pope weighed in. Rock endured hate mail from his in-group for years. But John Rock stuck to his conscience. He chose to help. Be John Rock.

I Don't Mean to Be Morbid

November 12, 2022

I have some better news but first an apology. I apologize. I don't mean to be morbid. I'm sorry if my thinking through hard things is distressing. That's not why I do it. Jordan and Jen both think I'm being a Debbie Downer. I'm not trying to be a downer when I tell you what I've found about my cancer. I myself am not feeling down from bad news. On the contrary, knowing the risks I face helps me focus on what I need to do. There is clarity in it. The Final Jeopardy song doesn't stress me. It tells me how much time I have to come up with an answer.

Here's the better news. Dr. Hope got back to me on my *FGFR2* mutation. She knew something I did not. Experts do that. While she agreed I wouldn't normally qualify for the drugs that target FGFR2 or qualify for most clinical trials, if my cancer does spread, she has another option. She said she could apply to my insurance company for "compassionate use" of the drugs. This means, she believes, that if my cancer were to spread—and we hope it does not spread—she may be able to get my insurance company to cover off-label treatments. These treatments could be the drugs that have some use against *FGFR2*-amplified tumors. She said she was able to get compassionate-use approval for another patient with my type of cancer.

Even more good news: A former colleague messaged me with a clinical trial for *FGFR2*-expressing tumors. I missed this trial because I was searching for gastric adenocarcinoma. This trial doesn't list gastric adenocarcinoma because the trial is testing a drug for any solid tumor that has my *FGFR2* amplification mutation. I read through the trial's exclusion criteria. I think I might qualify for this trial if my cancer spreads. I have asked Dr. Hope if her trained eye sees the same. The trial excludes other active cancers, but I don't think my cut-out kidney tumor counts as "active." This trial may be an option for me if my cancer spreads.

Back to the Final Jeopardy music. The main question is whether my cancer spreads. We hope that my surgery, my chemo, my immune system, and my upcoming radiation kill every last cancer cell. I think there is a 50% chance of that happening. Jen and Jordan favor the upper limit of 80%. Dr. Hope said she wasn't sure since she wasn't up on the *FGFR2* data. I sent her the paper. Oncologists must hate that. Either way, I know enough to drive myself to focus. If my cancer does spread, it will still be lethal. There may be additional treatments available to slow it down if it spreads. That's better news than I had yesterday.

Inspiration 54

Ask your doctor.

Most medical questions are hard for us to answer. There are so many ideas out there that sound like, maybe? Ask your doctor. After all, you pay them. For a doctor, most patient questions have one answer, and it's an easy answer. For them. To know the easy answer, it only takes four years of medical school and up to seven more years of residency. How about trusting your doctor over what your neighbor's cat saw on YouTube?

Inspiration 53

We don't pay experts to agree with us.

We learn nothing when we seek out experts who agree with us in our ignorance. Hire experts with the best credentials who are willing to explain things. Listen. Learn. Be excited to change your mind. Hire an expert to teach you what you don't want to learn the hard way. When you want validation, go to a parking garage.

Zap! Ow!

November 23, 2022

I had my third oxaliplatin infusion yesterday. I prepped my port site with a glob of anesthetic lidocaine. Much better. My cold sensitivity has gotten worse, though. It's now room-temperature sensitivity. Typing this is zapping me a bit. Touching the steering wheel. Zap. Walking on concrete in the garage in my socks. Zap, zap, zap. Washing my hands. Zap-fest. No more *Pulp Fiction*. Now it's *South Park*. Prying apart frozen tamales, oh, my gosh, I was like Cartman when he had an implanted V-chip that shocked him each time he swore. Zap, ow. But I want a tamale. Zap, ow. Zap, ow. Darn it! Zap, ow. I had to wear ski gloves.

Dr. Hope lowered my oxaliplatin dose by another 10%, since I was having such trouble. The nerve damage can be permanent if she goes too far with the chemo. Why does oxaliplatin cause cold sensitivity? Is there a way to treat it? I did some digging. I found out that in mice oxaliplatin messes up potassium channels on cold-sensing nerves. That's interesting. I have been having low potassium, which, in my mind, could be a one-two punch to these nerves. Ion channels are cellular switches for nerves. Messing up the potassium channels probably is like shorting out a light switch. Low potassium could drop the voltage. If so, I would think that more potassium might help me temporarily. I don't think it could help with anything permanent since the oxaliplatin damages the potassium channels, themselves. But adding in potassium could help the damaged ion channels work a bit better. At least for now, I'm thinking, adding potassium might make the zaps calm the heck down.

I didn't want to bring up mouse data with Dr. Hope—"I've never treated a mouse" and all that. I looked for papers on potassium in humans. I found a case study and sent it to Dr. Hope.

Here's what I messaged her:

> My neuropathy is markedly worse this cycle. My cold sensitivity is now room-temperature sensitivity. Even typing right now shocks my fingertips. My face also developed a "tight skin" feeling one gets with a mild sunburn (I have no sunburn) while I was in the infusion chair, and this has not resolved.
>
> I was doing some PubMed searches on the MOA of the cold sensitivity. I found a recent case study that reviewed the literature. www.ncbi.nlm.nih.gov/pmc/articles/PMC7360012/
>
> "Not all of the neurological symptoms observed during oxaliplatin-based treatment can be traced back directly to the oxaliplatin itself, and other factors, such as electrolyte imbalances, may contribute to the symptoms. Patients with gastro-intestinal malignancies are the patients most affected by neurotoxicity due to the side effects of chemotherapy and the disease itself."
>
> Intervention in the case study:
>
> "Following the discovery of low serum potassium levels, the patient was initially treated with a venous infusion of 20 mEq of KCl in 500 cc saline in a 1-h infusion, followed by treatment with oral potassium/ magnesium tablets (600 mg per tablet, roughly estimate of 8 mEq potassium per tablet). The patient was to continue taking the potassium/magnesium tablets after discharge from the hospital. At approximately 2 h after the initiation of the potassium endovenous infusion, the symptoms slowly subsided, and after another hour the patient's condition was back to normal and he could be discharged from the hospital."
>
> Question to you: Should I get additional supplemental potassium?

She agreed I should. She ordered potassium pills. I pick them up today. Hopefully they will help.

I *guess* I could also eat more bananas and potatoes. Dr. Hope sounds like my mother. I have limits.

Inspiration 52

Can they say *yes?*

Too often we ask for the wrong things from the wrong people. This frustrates them. This frustrates us. We get frustrated with the injustice of it all. We turn our ask into a rant. It's tempting to rant at customer support. What a waste. If they can't say *yes*, what's the point? What's true of a customer-support line is true of school, church, government, and work. Aim quickly at one target: What's in this person's power? Find it. Ask for it. What's outside their power? Don't toss away your time into that thicket. Can this person say *yes?* If not, ask for something else or get to someone who can say *yes*.

Inspiration 51

Accept the generosity of others.

Some of us find it hard to accept the generosity of others. When we are offered a gift, one that might embarrass us to accept, it helps if we recognize why we might feel uncomfortable. Sometimes we feel a gift is "charity," and taking charity means admitting we need charity. Good gifts given freely can make us feel as though we are failures. Rejecting a generous gift can be more about our egos than anything else. That's on us.

True, some people give generous gifts to feel superior. That's on them. Other times people give generous gifts because it makes them feel good. Sometimes people give gifts to make up for their shortcomings. A gift can be a sort of penance. It's good and right to help someone be a good giver by being an open-hearted receiver.

The best couples, I have noticed, are two good, generous people being generous givers and good receivers. They know they have good gifts to offer each other—time, talents, touch. Each receives those gifts without feeling made small.

How to Win Thanksgiving

November 24, 2022

Happy Thanksgiving! I started taking the potassium. I can't tell if it's helping. My hands are still pretty zappy.

If you haven't tried anything else, stop cooking the whole turkey intact. Either spatchcock it (remove the backbone and flatten the turkey) or go the whole way and break the bird down before cooking. Trust me. My turkey breasts used to be dry and terrible, and my turkey thighs used to be raw and terrible. Since I got into the backbone-ectomy business, my birds have been evenly cooked and juicy.

Problem this year: How do you cut up a cold turkey when you have to let go every five seconds to stop your hands from zapping? I was all ready to go with the Wüsthof carving knife I splurged on in a YOLO cancer moment. I had to give up before I got even one wing off. I'm lucky that my daughter Mallory is going for her nursing degree. She popped the joints and wielded the Wüsthof. Thanks, Mallory.

The others stepped up. Help can be had in a family of nine plus nephew Robert plus three live-in guests. The kids invited friends for dinner and games. We seated twenty at the table. I'm thankful we have a home where young people want to hang out. I think the general chaos helps make the place less intimidating. But, really, it's the kids. I am blessed with kind children. They are magnets. I get to be part of the big family I didn't grow up in. Our house is the hangout spot I never was invited to when I was young. There is probably a lesson there for fellow introverts.

Five Thanksgivings ago, I posted this on social media:

> How to Win Thanksgiving in Ten Easy Steps (when you disagree politically with your relatives).
>
> What's a "win"? You still love each other at the end. If your relatives believe propaganda, you make it easier for them to know the truth. That's a "win." It's not a successful defense of your political party. It's not a biting social media post to be shared. It's certainly not a CNN or FOX News bout of verbal professional wrestling.
>
> (1) SINCERELY love your relatives. If you are filled with rage at them, opening your mouth loses Thanksgiving. Don't play this year.
>
> (2) Don't blame victims of propaganda. OF COURSE, they believe nonsense. That's the point.
>
> (3) If they have nobody in daily life who believes what you do, stating your belief will be enough. They will disagree. That's okay. The simple realization that someone they care about thinks something different from what everyone else they know thinks is a BIG DEAL.
>
> (4) Ask them why they believe what they believe. Don't attack. Just listen. Usually, our understanding of others' beliefs is surprisingly shallow.
>
> (5) Use simple stories to illustrate points. Stories work. Arguments don't. Like that time Uncle John just gave the woman at the filling station "gas money" because he guessed she needed the money to feed her kids. (See?)
>
> (6) Make them laugh.

(7) Accept reasonable points even if they would undercut your beliefs. Being obstinate doesn't help anything. Heck, maybe you are wrong.

(8) Give them the information they can accept, which will always be less than all you know. Always. Don't pile on.

(9) If someone says, "Let's agree to disagree," that's it. Don't fight on.

(10) Know when you've won Thanksgiving. If you do convince someone of something, it sounds pretty mild. "Well, that's something to think about." You've won. Time for pie!

I didn't win Thanksgiving this year. I messed up. Jen was unhappy with my too-sweet maple glaze. That wasn't what I messed up. What I messed up wasn't at all sweet. I thought of a perfectly awful thing to say: "In five years, you can make it any way you want." I thought of it. I said it.

Annelise, age twelve, heard me. "That's messed up, Dad."

I could double down and blame cancer. I think I just did. Yeah, it was messed up. Sorry, family. Sometimes my holes dig holes.

This is going to sound odd, but I'm thankful for the Covid restrictions of the past three years. I know lockdowns have been a real hardship for many. For me, they have been a blessing separate from slowing down the pandemic. I got to live more with my family. We've been together in the same house for much of Covid. I've stopped wasting time in on-site client meetings and commutes. I've slept better in my own bed. I walk most days. My health is much improved (other than cancer, but you know what I mean). For everyone who helped keep Covid down in 2020 by staying home: Thank you. It could have been far, far worse. The hospitals really were being overwhelmed. You saved lives.

Inspiration 50

Own one good knife.

A high-quality chef's knife is the kitchen workhorse. You can use your chef's knife for almost everything. A chef's knife is the great big one the masked dude carries in a slasher film. Versatile.

You grip a chef's knife with your thumb and first finger at the base of the blade. The rest of your fingers curl around the handle. You are sure to cut your food-holding hand sooner or later if you put your fingers in the path of the blade. When chopping, that means you should use THE CLAW. The side of the knife can rest right against your clawed knuckles.

Dull knives are dangerous. Use a knife sharpener or whetstone every few months. Every meal prep, align the edge with a few slides down a sharpening steel (the metal rod thingy).

Inspiration 49

Don't overcomplicate meat.

Meat tastes great when cooked simply. This means simple seasonings and simple technique. Pat the meat dry. Season meat with coarse salt at least twenty minutes before cooking (overnight is better). I prefer garlic salt.

Add pepper now if you want it to stick (if the pepper burns on you, add at the end). Coat your pan using an oil with a high smoke point. Vegetable oil, bacon grease, and clarified butter all work great. Olive oil and butter straight out of the package burn. I usually use medium-high heat.

Brown your meat. The brown bits are from the Maillard reaction, a caramelization of protein and oil. The brown bits have the best taste. Don't crowd the pan, or whatever water remains won't evaporate quickly, and your meat will boil. Boiling water is too cold for the Maillard reaction. After your meat is brown, cook it to temperature (for thicker meat use the oven to cook through without burning).

Let your meat rest for at least twenty minutes before you cut into it.

Risk Adjusted

Bearded son-in-law: *How long did you work at Los Alamos?*

It was just a yearlong position in the theoretical biology group. I worked on the mathematics of virus transmission. This would come in handy twenty years later, when Covid hit.

I loved Los Alamos. The lab is in a small town like The Dalles but with PhDs like Princeton. Los Alamos is built on a series of mesas. You drive up and feel you've scaled the side of an aircraft carrier. There even is an airstrip running along the main mesa. Los Alamos is isolated. That's why it was chosen to be the hidden lab for the Manhattan Project that made the atomic bomb. I thought working there was cool. I liked my job. I got more papers out.

We left Los Alamos in 2000, when a fire nearly burned the town right down to the mesa tops. The Forest Service set the fire to thin the woods. It was not a good time of year to do that. Strong winds come through each year, and the strong winds did come through in 2000. The fire threatened to crest the hills into the townsite. We knew it was serious when military vehicles were at each major intersection. That's when they started telling everyone to get out, evacuate immediately. That was exciting and scary. I threw everything I could in the van. Jen went to get gas in our car. She had an exciting five hours trying to get back up the mesa. The military had the road blocked. She had my keys. I was stuck with the four kids until she got back. She ran a blockade to get us.

We holed up in a trailer house. We didn't have anything to do other than sit there and see if the entire town was going to burn. A lot of homes did burn, but the fire crews were able to save the lab and most of the town. It was a week of boredom and horror at the same time. That was also like Covid in a way.

I got my first titled job after Los Alamos. I was hired to be chief scientific officer at a place that said it was a venture capital firm investing in biotech. It was supposedly a well-financed investment fund. I later learned that wasn't so. The owner was similar to Trump in how he presented himself to the world. Whatever personality disorder Trump has, I've seen it before. I have absolutely seen it.

The unstoppable confidence not based on really anything.

It's not based on anything. "Did you see my name on that brick at the Seattle Opera?" (It was, in fact, the name of his father.) "Bill Gates and I are tight. He's borderline autistic. Did you know that?" My boss namedropped constantly. It took me far too long to figure out it was all a show. It's embarrassing.

You are not very skeptical. You were gullible, frankly.

I was naive. I started off a bit awestruck at his displays of wealth. We had a working waterfall in the office lobby. He drove a Harley-Davidson and a black Lincoln. He wore designer shirts with French cuffs. He was on Gonzaga's board of regents. He talked often of the wealth he said he had made in shopping malls and oil. Lunchtime he paged through catalogues for private jets. He talked about his vacations in Lake Tahoe, this place, that place. Talk, talk, talk. Scientists are not trained to detect liars. Mistakes? Yes. Lies? No. I didn't see through it.

For what it's worth, I wasn't the only one he fooled. He had some investors. He lunched with politicians. Reporters would call to quote his opinion on local business news. He convinced the publicly traded medical technology company Heartport to offer him equity to stave off their NASDAQ delisting. (This didn't work, and he admitted publicly he never bought 5% of Heartport stock; he only filed SEC paperwork claiming he had.)

My job was to figure out which biotech inventions made investment sense. Some of the university inventions we were looking at didn't seem to make scientific sense to me. Those were easy. The harder problem was valuing the inventions that did make scientific sense. I didn't know how much the inventions were worth. I started doing the normal academic approach. I looked up papers. How much is a biotech asset worth? Nobody knew. The field was too new. Even in the best journal, *Nature Biotechnology,* investment professionals would say they set a price on biotech companies by counting their PhDs, counting their patents, or adding up their lab floor space. These are all insane. I couldn't believe anyone admitted this in print. These things in no way have much to do with the actual value of a biotech company.

A biotech's value is in its pipeline drugs. How much are they worth? Our chief financial officer showed me the net present value equation. Net present value is based on the idea that money's worth more today than it's worth in the future. It makes sense. But I thought NPV was not enough to figure out biotech valuations. Pipeline drugs are risky assets. Drugs have to pass clinical trials. Clinical trials are pass/fail tests. If a trial passes, the drug continues. If a trial fails, it's all over. What I thought we needed was to put the clinical-trial risks into the NPV equation.

So I did that. I worked out the math. I decided to call it rNPV, risk-adjusted net present value. I wrote it up and published it in *Nature Biotechnology.* It got attention immediately. I got asked to attend the Milken Institute's Global Conference, which is a mini-Davos. My equation got written up by The Motley Fool investment advisors. Later, when I was a student in business school, I got sent a friend's homework from UCLA. His homework assignment read, "What would Jeff Stewart think about this investment?" Surreal. That rNPV equation is now the most used valuation method in biotech.

Even though we had an equation to price out biotech assets to buy, there didn't seem to be venture capital in our company to spend. The owner stopped paying bills. He liked to use speakerphone, and I remember when one caller screamed over speakerphone, "Where is my money?" This was all strange to me because he was still portraying himself as ultrawealthy. Then paychecks started bouncing. The owner blamed his personal banker.

I stuck it out as long as I could. I hoped to help get the company in a better spot for investors and get my back pay. Eventually, the owner declared bankruptcy. I was out of work. Jobs dried up. We had just entered the dot-com bust. I never got my back pay.

Being out of work is the pits. I felt worthless. I did get some work-for-hire as a consultant. A biotech company in Canada asked me to do rNPV for them. I did it for peanuts because I didn't know how much biotechs would pay. Did I charge $3,000? I might have. These things are regularly sold for, at a minimum, $75,000 and more like $150,000 to $300,000. I've learned a lot since then. I do that work for my company now.

Jen convinced me to go to business school at Notre Dame. With scholarships and student loans, we could just make it, financially, even with a fifth child, Carissa. I did think an MBA program would be two things: lame and easy. I was wrong. Business school was not lame, and it was not easy.

You were proven wrong.

Totally wrong. I was so arrogant. Business school was really hard and really interesting. I loved my investment classes. I took venture capital classes because I wanted to be in venture capital for real this time.

Not for some, you know, scumbag.

I found out at graduation my former employer had tried to pressure Notre Dame into expelling me—I assume to get me to drop my pursuit of back pay. His pressure backfired. The dean told me as much. I know people can change, but based on calls I got from those suing my former boss before he died, he didn't change.

Notre Dame had the nicest people. The students were nice. The teachers were nice. I was a good student again. I took the super-hard classes, and the super-hard teachers liked me. I played on the university trivia team. I was half the player I had been, but we still got ninth at nationals.

In my second year, I was the teaching assistant for microeconomics and was offered the job of research assistant for the applied investment management professor. I was making a little bit more money tutoring first-year students. Child number six, Mallory, was going to be born just after graduation. I needed that tutoring money. I should have taken the research assistant position anyway. The professor had written a leading investment textbook and served on major investment analyst boards. The assistantship with him would have been a career builder. Live and learn.

The students I tutored must have said good things about me. At graduation, the dean started talking about one student who was a "superhero" who saved others from failing. He was talking about me. He called me up to win the Dean's Award. I was shocked. I didn't realize they saw me that way. I was just trying to make some money on the side. It felt so affirming after having such a depressing experience at Princeton. My parents were surprised. Jen said she felt vindicated.

There was one terrible time at Notre Dame. While Jen was pregnant with Mallory, we got the call from Jen's father that her younger brother Rod had committed suicide. I didn't do the right thing for Jen. I was mad at Rod. I was mad at him for hurting Jen. I was mad at him for hurting his parents. I didn't think about him as being depressed. I don't know why I didn't. I just thought of him as being selfish. I didn't go to the funeral. I stayed in Indiana and did my classes. Jen had to travel from South Bend to New Jersey and face Rod's death alone. There is nothing I've done I regret more. I should have known better. I did know better. I did it anyway.

Notre Dame was the last time I was a student. I spent eleven years in colleges. I've since avoided Princeton's campus even though work has often taken me to the town. Bad memories. I still feel them whenever I drive past the gates. My breath catches. You'd think it would have gone away by now. It's like the bullies. They can't hurt me now, but my body doesn't know that. Notre Dame, in contrast, relaxes me. I find myself smiling when I think of the teachers, the gold-leaf dome, Touchdown Jesus, even the winter wind cutting across the parking lot. Notre Dame feels like safety. I left Notre Dame feeling replenished and ready for a career.

Inspiration 48

Many fall for false wealth.

The two billionaires I've personally known got there the wrong way. One is in prison for fraud. The other is a Russian oligarch and outside US law. They had real billions, but their secret wasn't anything to imitate.

Many keep up a false appearance of wealth—beach houses, ski vacations, new BMWs—but there is nothing there. It's not wealth. It's a pile of unpaid bills. We can't tell who is legitimately wealthy from the show they make. Don't waste your time, as I did, trying to figure out their secret.

The most common sources of actual wealth are inheritance and business ownership—often in normal businesses like car dealerships or beverage distributors.

Inspiration 47

Leave liars.

Most people who believe nonsense aren't dumb. They trust bad sources. It takes work to scrub our brains of fake facts. We'd have been better off learning nothing than learning lies. The most important single thing we do to learn these days is to walk away from bad sources. Before trusting any articles, any videos, any talking heads, conduct a background check. What reason do you have to believe these sources know what they are talking about? Are they paid to say what they are telling you? Do they win awards (a good sign), or do they fail fact-checks (a bad one)? Do they admit when they get things wrong? When you detect a source is lying, don't waste your time sifting their other words for nuggets. Leave liars. When you find sources that prove to be trustworthy, stick with them. Even then, don't stop checking for credibility. People change. So do companies. Sometimes credible sources drift from reality when they leave their field of expertise.

Tuna Are Impossible

November 25, 2022

I'm pretty wiped out today. Night chills are back. I had to break out my electric blanket again. I'm going to hang out in bed, watch YouTube, and lose at chess.

Why am I not losing my hair? I don't know. Oxaliplatin is chemotherapy but doesn't usually make patients bald. Why not? Why does other chemo cause hair loss but mine doesn't? I wasn't able to figure it out. I spent an hour reading journal articles with no luck. The scientific literature is light on mechanism. I can find which chemotherapies have that side effect. I can find what can be done to slow the hair loss. There are wearable scalp refrigerators that slow circulation and keep some of the infused chemo from really hitting the hair follicles. Clever. The efficacy is pretty darn good. I'll ask for the scalp refrigerator if I get stronger chemo. I still can't find any paper that tells me why one versus another chemo causes hair loss. It's puzzling. I asked Dr. Hope. She didn't know either. Science is fun that way. It doesn't take much to find a question nobody knows the answer to.

Why does the full moon look so large on the horizon but not so much when it's high in the sky? We didn't know the answer twenty-five years ago. It turns out that when we don't have a frame of reference, our mind has to guess at how far away something is. We see the moon high in the sky, and our mind takes a guess. The problem is we guess the moon is closer than it actually is. Our mind guesses the moon is far away but not *that* far. Based on how close we think the moon is, we can tell the moon must be large but not nearly as large as it really is. When we see the moon on the horizon, we can finally tell the moon is cosmically far away. So our mind knows the moon has to be a lot larger. Cool, no?

Twenty-five years ago, we also didn't know how insects fly. Seriously. Insects' wings are too small. The math on the lift doesn't work. Do the math, and insects can't fly. Yet they fly. Then this guy made a working model of a dragonfly, put his dragonfly model in mineral oil, and just watched the thing. Isn't that delightful? He watched the wings and the oil and saw what was happening for the first time. His model dragonfly wings made little cyclones of oil. The cyclones spun and gave the wings the extra lift. And that's how insects fly.

Same sort of thing happened with tuna. Tuna are fishy torpedoes. A tuna can swim fifty miles per hour. That's five times as fast as the fastest human can run. Tuna are impossible. The math doesn't work out. By testing model fish, researchers found that tuna swim fast by making little whirlpools and flicking them left and right with their tails. The whirlpools shoot tuna in the tail. Tuna jet through the water on, well, waterjets.

What the heck is in the middle of saliva? I wet my fingers and pull them apart slowly, and there is a thread in the middle. The water forms beads on the thread like pearls on a necklace. What makes that thread? I don't know. I don't know that anyone knows. Is the thread the enzyme amylase? Mucin glycoprotein? Loose DNA? It looks like the DNA "snot ball" we make in molecular biology labs with phenol extraction. That's an unanswered question—at least to me—literally at our fingertips.

What does a protein feel like? I want to know. Pharma companies spend hundreds of millions of dollars every year making crystals of proteins so we can take X-ray pictures of them. We know a lot about what proteins do from looking at them. But how much more could we know if we could feel proteins? What if we could hold proteins in our hands and play with them? Think how different it is to be looking at a pocketknife versus playing with the darn thing. Or a bicycle. Or a can opener. Watson and Crick figured out the structure of DNA from making a cardboard model they could play with. I desperately want real-time computational feedback on what a protein feels like. I want to play with proteins. There are haptic, force-feedback gloves for protein docking. We can feel how two proteins might fit together. But every time I've looked for protein-*folding* haptics, I find nothing. We have to be close. We have haptics. We have protein-folding algorithms. Someone has to put those two together (with, I expect, some blazing-fast computers). This is a freebie to anyone into computers and molecular biology: Make a general haptic model of protein folding. Let us touch proteins with our own two hands. You'll change the world. I can feel it.

Inspiration 46

A job is a kind of giving.

A job isn't just a paycheck. When we work, we are performing an act of service. When we work, we are giving to others. We are giving our time. We are giving our talents. We are helping. Yes, we are paid in return. That doesn't take from what we give. Giving through work is as real as any other giving. Work will be how we spend most of our lives. We're happier when we see work for the giving it is.

Inspiration 45

"No, you said . . ." is the dumbest argument.

Communication has four parts: what was intended, what was said, what was heard, and what was understood. Communication can break down at any of these four parts. Unless there is a recording, neither you nor anyone else will know where the communication breakdown was. There was a miscommunication. Leave it at that.

Chemobrain

November 29, 2022

Daylight saving time ended this month. I looked out my window at 5:00 P.M., and it was already dark. You know how the days seem suddenly short? This chemo round is shortening my world. I'm good for a while, and then I'm not. I'm spending a lot of time in bed. My day is done. My lamp is low. My taper is thin. I just need to sleep. I find myself dreading my morning meetings. They could burn my whole day.

I sent what I've written so far to Sam the Statistician, my coauthor from Princeton. He's ninety-two. I wanted him to read it, and, well, why take chances? According to the Social Security Administration, the life expectancy of a ninety-two-year-old man is about four years. He says he sleeps a lot these days. Same, Sam, same.

My hand and foot pain would just be a good story if I knew the pain was going to be temporary. If getting zapped for another month is the worst thing chemo does to me, I'll count that as a blessing. My worry is that I might always feel this pain. It's worse each chemo round. One of my oncologists said they push the infused chemo as much as they can. "As much as they can" seems to mean "until things go terribly wrong." They keep asking if I'm getting chest pain or if my throat is closing up. I gather that would be terribly wrong. I don't like watching anyone stand next to a cliff edge. I feel as if I'm walking right along the edge. We won't know we've gone too far until we go too far.

A client project I was supposed to start got an FDA delay until January. I usually am excited to start a new project. When there is a delay, I get frustrated that I have to wait to chase the tennis ball. This time all I felt was relief. My relief was short-lived. Two days later I had forgotten about the delay. My team had to remind me. It completely slipped my mind.

Chemotherapy does that. There are 142 articles on PubMed with "chemobrain" in the title. Chemobrain is a loss of memory and executive function. Executive function means focus, planning, decision-making, and problem-solving. Executive function is what we think of when we think of thinkers.

Welcome to chemobrain. I'm feeling it.

Thinking is my job. It would be one thing to have that thinking done in private. My thinking is live on stage. Client meetings have a performance aspect. It's an intimate show. Client audiences often comprise a member of the company C-suite plus a squad of mid-level executives. For every slide I craft a story. People think in stories. The best presentations use numbers, tables, and graphs as characters in a story. When I present, I'm working out live what story can be told. I improvise. It's like live jazz. Usually, I'm good at it. I think (hope) I'm the only one noticing that I'm usually better at this. I'm still performing, but I don't have as many performances in me each day. My post-performance crashes are hard.

Thinking is much of what makes me *me*. Chemo makes it harder to think. Chemo is damaging my nerves. A brain is made of nerves. I've known what it's like to lose my ability to think. I never want that again. There is something about sitting in that chemo chair or shaking out the twice-a-day pills that is harder for me than most hard things. I told the kids it reminded me of the cursed potion in *Harry*

Potter and the Half-Blood Prince. Immersed in the potion was a horcrux holding a piece of Voldemort's soul. It had to be destroyed. To do that, Dumbledore had to drink every drop of the potion. Each drop took something of Dumbledore away. He lost his strength. He lost his courage. He lost his mind. He begged. He moaned. He became pathetic.

It's a bit pathetic to compare oneself to Albus Dumbledore. I blame the chemo.

Inspiration 44

Every slide is a story.

You may have heard that a speaker shouldn't read slides verbatim. Good advice. But what should a speaker do instead? The speaker's job is to tell the story illustrated by the slides. There are two kinds of slides—slides with too many things to fit in the same story and slides with too few things to tell a story at all. If there are too many things on the slide, the story you tell will start the same: "What's important on this slide is . . ." When there are too few things on the slide, your job is to fill in the missing setting, character, or plot. Every slide has a story. Tell the story.

Inspiration 43

Character assassination has no place in marriage.

In marriage, argument is normal. A marriage will survive complaints. A marriage may not survive character assassination. Instead of complaining about something narrow—my pet peeve is a cluttered walkway—we train our verbal weapons on our spouse's character. "You think only of yourself." "You can't handle money." "You must have a guilty conscience." Character assassination isn't "being honest." Character assassination isn't "airing things out." Character assassination is a personal attack. Character assassination does nothing positive. Character assassination doesn't bring us the change we want.

Oh, and don't give your spouse the silent treatment either. You're not taking the high ground with silence. Read John Gottman's evidence-based book *The Seven Principles for Making Marriage Work* for more. It's excellent.

A Little Experiment

December 1, 2022

I think the potassium pills helped.

Remember the case study where extra potassium helped a patient with the zappy chemo neuropathy? Dr. Hope prescribed me potassium pills. I couldn't tell at first that they were working.

I ran out of potassium pills two days ago. Dr. Hope prescribed only a week's worth. I'm not 100% sure she wasn't trying to run a little experiment on me. Accidental or not, her experiment worked.

My last potassium day, I was medium zappy. Room temperature hurt if I drummed my fingers. Cold zapped me good, but the pain was dying down. I was starting to put down the Gatorade and add some ice to my Diet Coke. My zappy pain got worse yesterday. It's way worse today even though I didn't take more oxaliplatin. Every other oxaliplatin infusion, my finger pain started bad, then eased off. Today, zappy is back. Zappy is not happy. I'm feeling the burn even while I wear gloves.

I'm zappy, but I'm also getting more energy. My sleep has improved. I resumed my daily walks. I'm starting to enjoy work again. Good timing. I kick off a cardiology project next Monday and deliver on an ADHD project next Friday.

I even had the energy to shine my attention headlights on a client presentation and give high-beam feedback. Capitalize generic drug names the same way you'd capitalize "pencil." Hyphenate "X-chromosome inactivation" (adjective) but not "she had two X chromosomes" (noun). Genes get italics, but proteins don't. And, no, there were not 19 billion anticoagulant patients in the United States last year. Don't stop thinking, people.

I feel confident my copy editor (my wife) is going to have to go back through past chapters on *FGFR2* genes and FGFR2 proteins and undo her edits. Right, Jen?

I asked Dr. Hope to prescribe more potassium chloride—this time the liquid, not the horse pills. The liquid should give better absorption.

December 3, 2022

I don't know what camel urine tastes like. But I have a hard time imagining camel urine tasting as bad as fifteen milliliters of liquid potassium chloride.

On the plus side, no more zappy chemo neuropathy. One day of liquid potassium chloride, and I've gone from getting tased through my ski gloves to guzzling Diet Coke with ice.

Camel urine works like a charm.

Inspiration 42

When others don't know what you know, it means you're needed.

Sometimes we get annoyed when others don't know how to do something we've mastered. How could they not know this? It's so easy! We can get frustrated with them. When others don't know what we know, it means we are needed. It's a good thing. We all need to be needed.

Inspiration 41

Yes, you can do the job better. That's not the manager's job.

Many new managers are promoted because they are the best at doing the job. It makes sense. But it's also a problem. New managers' high skill levels hold them back. It's perverse. New managers want to do the work. New managers know if they do the job, it will be done right. When this is you, remember that your job is not to do the work. Your job is to get your team to do the work. Your team has to learn. The only way this can happen is if you stop doing what got you into management in the first place. That's not an easy thing to ask of a successful doer. But that's the job. You'll have to find self-fulfillment in mentoring your team and seeing them learn.

The same thing is true of raising children.

Con Artists

December 4, 2022

Antivaxxers heard I have cancer. Can you guess what they said caused it?

I figured this would be coming sooner or later. I've put myself out there as a target. I have been vocal in The Dalles about Covid vaccination. It was front-page news that I volunteered for the Pfizer Covid vaccine trial. When Covid misinformation was rampant, I spent every bit of my local fame from winning on *Jeopardy!* to undo Covid lies.

One hometown antivaxxer tagged me on social media: "As an original Pfizer trial victim, with three types of cancer, you should know better. Or at least be questioning why it happened! We have to stop the lunacy."

I'm trying to appeal to her sense of human decency. That may work. I don't think she thinks of herself as someone who exploits cancer patients.

Another antivaxxer posted: "Renowned Oncologist Warns of Cancers Rapidly Progressing in 'Boosted' People," and pointed out that my cancer was diagnosed after I was vaccinated.

There is a fair question to ask: What caused my cancer? How do we know it's not the Covid vaccine?

A lot of things cause gastric cancer. If I had a genetic disease, that would be clear. Otherwise, the cause could be anything that messes up DNA. What does that?

I've been exposed to many DNA-mutating agents. I worked with probable carcinogens on our farm and with known carcinogens in molecular biology labs. I worked at one nuclear weapons lab and lived downstream from another. I repaired thousands of radiators with lead solder. I've flown in enough airplanes to be hit with more than my share of cosmic rays. I eat bacon. *H. pylori* causes gastric cancer, and I could have been infected with that ulcer-causing bacterium any time over my fifty years. I once tasted a carcinogen during a college chemistry exam. I had thought the sample was salt substitute and wanted to confirm. Funny, it didn't taste like salt. It burned. (Uh oh.) I had put mercuric chloride on my own tongue. I spent some quality time that afternoon at the lab wash station.

From my training, I know what did *not* cause my cancer. I know it the same way we all know that rock and roll music didn't start a house fire. That's not how fire works. Whatever caused my cancer could not have been a Covid vaccine. That's not how Covid vaccines work. Covid vaccines can't change our DNA. Covid vaccine mRNA doesn't even make it to the nuclei, where DNA lives. My Covid injection site wasn't anywhere near my tumors. There is no physical way for my Covid vaccine to have mutated the DNA in my stomach or kidney.

That's where theory gets us. What about evidence? There is a heaping pile of clinical evidence that Covid vaccines do not cause cancer. My massive Pfizer clinical trial found no cancer risk. Follow-on monitoring of thirteen billion doses detected side effects that were so rare they arose in fewer than one in one hundred thousand. Even ultra-rare risks would have shown up. Cancer didn't. There is no cancer risk.

Covid vaccines are here and gone. The only thing a Covid vaccine leaves behind is protection. What about side effects years in the future? That's a fantasy. No vaccine *ever* has had a side effect show up more than forty-five days after injection. If there is a side effect—even a rare one—it's already happened, and we know about it.

Antivaxxers try to spook us into fear of the unknown. But the vaccines aren't unknown. We know vaccines very well. The Covid vaccines are the most studied in history. However, it takes real effort to learn vaccine science. Watching YouTube doesn't cut it. It takes years of study from credible sources. There is no shortcut. Immunology is the deep end of the deep end of molecular biology. Not many swim there. I have. The evidence, as I understand it, is overwhelming. My Covid vaccine did not cause my cancer.

I don't have much of a temper. Yet my anger burns white-hot for Covid con artists. Covid con artists tricked hundreds of thousands into death by suffocation. Think about that. Take it in. Think of how horrible it would be to trick even one person into struggling to breathe for a single hour. Or a day. Or a week. Or the rest of a too short life. Average life expectancy in the US dropped by two years over the Covid pandemic. Those who crafted the Covid cons were not dumb. They were smart. They misused their smarts to fool those who misplaced their trust in them. The Covid con artists were talented, well-spoken liars. Why did they do it? Money. Money and fame. Covid con artists made—are still making—fortunes by selling treatments that don't work for Covid. When these con artists aren't profiting off false hope, they are preening on television and Joe Rogan.

It's gross.

Inspiration 40

Evil dresses nice.

Evil is more effective when it's hard to spot. Evil will dress up in nice clothing. Evil will wear makeup. Evil will sound smart. Smart evil doesn't show its horns. This is not to say we should distrust everyone who bathes. Most well-spoken people are not evil. Just don't be surprised when evil "seemed so nice." Of course, it did.

Inspiration 39

Propaganda victims are victims. Don't blame victims.

We are awash in propaganda. The propaganda is swept over us by foreign powers, political machines, and even Macedonian teenagers looking to make a buck on Google ads. We may find ourselves frustrated when friends and family fall for propaganda. Let that frustration go. Propaganda victims are victims. Don't blame victims. Instead, rescue them from the filthy water. You have an asset no propagandist has. You have shared a real life with your real friends and your real family. Real life is your currency. Spend it. Spend it on them. Bring them bits of truth. It might take a while. They won't believe you at first, but they will know you mean well. It's like a tangled knot of hair. You have to pick at it. Redeem your own. After all, who else is going to do it?

Not Even Pretending to Fight

December 6, 2022

"You're going to fight that cancer." No, I'm really not.

I get unreasonably irritated when I hear that I'm going to "fight that cancer." What's my weapon? Harsh language? What good would fighting (whatever that means) do? I'm not going to fight cancer. I'm not going to beat cancer. I'm not going to lose my battle with cancer either. I don't even think my good attitude or bad one is going to do much of much, at least so far as fighting cancer goes.

The actual cancer fight looks like this. Oxaliplatin is spot-welding my DNA so the replicating DNA strands snarl in a tangled mess. The oral 5-FU prodrug is keeping new DNA pieces from being made and poisoning whatever DNA manages to copy itself despite the oxaliplatin welding. My immune system is hunting down stray cancer cells that survive the war chemo is waging on my DNA. In three months, chest radiation will blow double-stranded breaks in my DNA—mortal molecular wounds. If the actual fighters kill every last cancer cell, then I live. If even one cancer cell lives, I die.

I'm not a fighter. I'm the battlefield.

Who is being reassured here anyway? Is this what makes others comfortable—

imagining cancer patients fighting on the front lines? Is this what is expected of us? Dress up like Civil War cosplayers? Load our muskets with blanks? Stand still for our portrait? What a waste. I refuse to play the part.

I'm not fighting. I'm not even pretending to fight. I know that may be distressing to people who care about me. I'm sorry, truly. I'm not finding the energy to pretend. Instead, I'm trying to live the best life I can with whatever time I have. There are some things only I can do. Nobody else can catch up with my old friend Sam the Statistician for me. Nobody else can be Annelise's father reading her *The City of Gold and Lead.* Nobody else can draw up a list of my online accounts and passwords. Nobody else can be my wife's husband (at least not yet). Nobody else can write this message in a bottle—the words I cast out to be exhumed from the sand with, I hope, a bit of wonder in the finding. That should be enough. I want it to be enough.

I know it's not enough.

Inspiration 38

Sometimes we are better at fighting for others.

It can be hard for some of us to fight for ourselves. We avoid conflict. We don't want to be seen as pushy. It's easier to fight for a good cause. It's easier to fight for others. Remember that you are not just one person alone with no ties to anyone else. You have people you care about and who care about you. Sometimes a fight for yourself is really a fight for them. When you have trouble advocating for yourself, consider how your friends or family will be harmed if you fail to fight. Some of us finally find our strength when we recognize we fight for others.

Inspiration 37

Negotiate interests, not rights.

"It's my right!" We can gnaw on injustice as though it's a bone we're trying to crack for marrow. "It's my right. It's my right." We can act as if it's an incantation that will do something if we think it enough times in a row. In negotiation, there's a better way. Set your rights to the side for a moment. They'll be there when you get back. During negotiations, focus on interests. What's in your interest? What's in their interest? Negotiate from interests—what makes your situation better—and you'll get more of what you want. You know what else will happen? You won't stew as much. You'll be happier with the deal you negotiate.

While we are on the topic of negotiation, you need a BATNA. BATNA stands for best alternative to negotiated agreement. When you get an offer, compare it to your next-best option. This is where a BATNA is powerful. You can be honest with the other side. You'd like to accept the offer, but your BATNA is better. You end up collaborating with the counterparty to get their offer improved until you would be an idiot not to say *yes*. What if you have no good alternative? Don't negotiate yet. Go get a BATNA. Then start negotiating.

Love Your Client

December 10, 2022

Yesterday was a pretty okay Friday. I'm on my chemo holiday week. Jen and I went on our first date in months. I get zapped only when I'm actually holding ice. I feel healthy. My thinking has regained its edge.

My consulting team had our final delivery Friday for a CEO with a pediatric mental health treatment. The CEO was my favorite kind of client: critical.

You read right. CEOs who are critical, even rude, are my favorite clients. It's easy to win them over. You just have to deliver great work. There's a cleanness to the task.

It's a terrible sort of job to be the CEO of a life-science company. Success can mean life for patients, and failure, death. Think of the pressure. That success is out of the CEO's control. Success in biopharma is mostly the luck of having started down the right river. There is no map. The CEO is shooting rapids in a barrel that could either end its voyage on the shores of Lake Placid or more abruptly in a splintered mass at the base of Niagara Falls. The barrel is taking on water. There is more bailing than steering. The CEO is bailing in front of an audience. Every meeting with investors, board members, or employees is a bailout performance. I know the feeling of every act being a public performance.

It's exhausting. Add to the performance pressure that a lot of CEOs—especially scientist types—expect management consultants to be kind of scammy. The old joke is that, if you ask a management consultant what time it is, the consultant borrows your watch, tells you the time, then keeps the watch.

Put a CEO in a kickoff meeting, and before slide three, consultants can find themselves called to the floor for an impromptu duel. The CEO draws steel by challenging everything: every assumption, every data point, every claim. The CEO wins satisfaction by revealing the consultant to be Making Stuff Up. The consultant cannot win this duel. Winning is losing. And losing is losing. The best the consultant can do is to survive without either side drawing blood. The duel ends only when the CEO concedes the consulting team has delivered real insights. There is a danger zone when consultants don't yet have those real insights. We have to rush past the danger zone. Only with the first physician interview, the first financial analysis, or the first solid piece of science can the CEO choose to make a consultant an advisor, not a pincushion.

Until we have earned trust, I have to remind myself and my team to love our clients. Love them. Serve them. I think it's the best way to consult. Yes, the CEO is attacking us. Love anyway. Never forget that we serve them. How do we turn the other cheek and give them our cloak as well?

Only once we deliver great work do we flip the critical client. Delivery is what it takes to win. That pattern of behavior makes the critical client my favorite client. We deliver, and we earn trust. The CEO stops sparring and starts listening. That's what happened this Friday. We delivered on the project. We gave the client good news from physicians and earned the right to give hard news on insurance coverage. We delivered, and the client was well served.

Chemo Monday.

Inspiration 36

Respect must be earned.

I have a hard time believing that anyone who demands respect gets actual respect. Are we trying to raise respectful kids or convincing liars? We are soothing our own scraped egos when we demand respect for ourselves. Kids pick up on that.

Showing respect to others, on the other hand, is good and right. Kids pick up on that too. Even though demanding respect for ourselves is doomed to fail, we can teach kids to respect others. Modeling works. Teaching kids why others have earned our respect helps our kids feel that respect. This is especially true when we teach our kids to respect our spouse. We relieve our spouse of the futile task of demanding respect.

Inspiration 35

Love your client.

The first week of training, I tell new consults at work to "love your client." Bad consultants view clients as adversaries. Bad consultants mock clients behind their backs. Bad consultants exploit. I teach new consultants never to do any of that. Instead, I teach them, "Love your client. Just love them. We serve them." It's corny, but it's true. When we love those whom we serve, even hard work for challenging people becomes a joy. I think it's impossible to serve people well and not love them. "Love your client" is the lesson consultants tell me they remember years later.

Indoor Pet

December 12, 2022

Chemo today. The Duke nurses are cycling through arm-high stacks of pagers as though this is The Cheesecake Factory.

The cancer center clientele is nothing I've seen at The Cheesecake Factory, not even at early-bird dinner. Every third guest has a cane, walker, or wheelchair. I'm the youngest one with a pager. Most of us have assistants: husbands, wives, adult children. I know I'd have a waiting list of family willing to come along. I don't want an audience. When I'm not feeling well, I just want to be alone and lick my wounds. I'm like a hurt pet.

I used to be an outdoor pet. That changed after grad school. Now I'm an indoor pet. I barely expose myself to the weather. I live in North Carolina, which means that unless the HVAC fails, the weather is the same every season, every day: 72 degrees Fahrenheit, wind speed of overhead fan. I'm a man for one season. I wonder what my ancestors would think of me. I don't have to wonder long. They would think I'm soft.

Oops. There's my pager. Guess my table is ready.

———

I'm back from port prep and blood draws.

The best book I've read for public performance is *Speaking Shakespeare*. It teaches more than acting. *Speaking Shakespeare* helps free the voice for talking, singing, presenting to clients. The book reminds us how physically fit the average person was four hundred years ago. Everyone walked everywhere. A fistfight was unremarkable. Theirs was a physical world. They carried swords. Our ancestors' core strength had to have been incredible even though their nutrition was terrible. They were scarred tomcats, scrappy. Don't try to pet them. Think what that fitness did to the voice. Even untrained, they must have spoken with power. Think what softness is in our voices. I hear it in the consultants I train. They run out of breath. They trail off into the creak of vocal fry. I no longer have the strength of living outdoors. I have to prep my voice for the mic.

"Aggressive behavior will not be tolerated" reads a banner on the chemo infusion floor. Sign of the times. While I wait with my second pager of the day, this one for Dr. Hope, a patient in the waiting room is holding court about Donald Trump. "He never said to suspend the Constitution. It was just a small number of people in the Capitol. D.C. was already burning. Now they're held in solitary confinement without trial."

There's my second pager.

I'm back again. As I left the waiting room, I chose to say one thing: "Trump didn't call for the Constitution's 'suspension.' He called for its 'termination.'"

"The Constitution is already suspended anyway," the patient called out to my back. "We don't have a First Amendment anymore." He said it, I note, without anyone stopping him.

I worry I've raised my kids too easy. They may be indoor pets too. It probably will sound off to you, but when I think what might happen if I were to die from this, I get a bit excited about the possibilities for my kids. My exiting the stage will give them a reason to head out of the house. They will get out and explore. I'm fine with that.

No third pager. No more infused chemo. Dr. Hope decided the zappy neuropathy was getting dangerous. I will keep taking oral chemo for another cycle or two.

Ta-ta for now. This isn't goodbye.

Inspiration 34

Quit.

Some problems are not solvable. We wait too long to quit. This isn't just speculation. Quitting has been tested. When people didn't know if they should quit—where it was such a close call that they let a coin flip decide—the quitters ended up happier than non-quitters. What's the lesson? We stick out bad situations too long. Quit sooner. Quit more often. Be happier. When we don't know what to do, when we think it's a close call, it's not a close call. It's an easy choice. Quit.

Sometimes we need to walk around the corner to find we're on a dead end. Quitting can be an informed choice to do something better.

My favorite saying is from Turkey: "No matter how far you've gone down the wrong road, turn back!"

I guess they call it Türkiye, now.

Inspiration 33

The law is about rules, not common sense.

I hope this never happens to you, but if you believe you are under suspicion for a crime, say nothing until you speak to a lawyer. Common sense is great for most things. The law isn't one of them. The law is about rules. Those rules come from the Constitution, written laws, court cases, rules in rule books, and even plain old tradition. Just accept that the law won't always be what you think it is. The law definitely is not what you think it should be. If you aren't a lawyer, there is roughly a 0% chance you know how the rules work. Listen to your lawyer.

Will I Live Through You?

December 16, 2022

I'd like to live forever just without all the fuss. I don't want to be forgotten. I've come to realize that's why I'm writing.

I'm trying to live on in my kids' minds. I want to leave them with my mental tools to pull out when they need. My words are my tools. I keep them in my mental kit. I've assembled complete sets. I've kept my tools sharp and oiled. I want them to be used. The philosopher Ludwig Wittgenstein said, "The limits of my language are the limits of my world." I want my language to live on in my kids. I want them to carry my world with them.

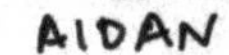

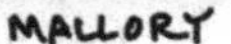

H. L. Davis is the only Pulitzer Prize–winning novelist from Oregon. He's from The Dalles. For my whole childhood, I never heard of H. L. Davis. All eighteen years I spent growing up, all my time in English class and the Wasco County Public Library, never once did I see his novel *Honey in the Horn*. There is no H. L. Davis Elementary in The Dalles. Instead, my hometown has an elementary school named for the army colonel who hanged Native Americans who had surrendered under a white flag. We remember him. In our high school is a shrine to sports. The glass case holds the state-championship trophies that teach students how they will be remembered or forgotten by their world. There are leather football helmets worn more than a century ago.

CARISSA

"Writing is therapeutic for him," Jen told friends and family. She said that until I asked her to stop. I didn't know why at first, but when I overheard her, what I felt was rage. I was surprised at how angry I got. "I'm not writing for therapy," I told myself. If I need therapy, I should just get therapy. Instead of writing for therapy, I should be doing anything else with anyone else. If spending this time writing is therapy, what a waste.

JESSICA

What I told myself is that I want to help. I want to help my kids. I want to help anyone who reads this. I want to help you. I do feel satisfied when people tell me that reading early drafts of this book helped them understand what their own parents had gone through with cancer. Not everyone wants to talk about cancer with their kids.

But if I'm honest, my writing is less noble. It's not even therapy. My writing is my bid to take more than my allotted hour. I'm trying to live past my time. I'm worried I might not get enough. I'm trying to throw my body astride the calendar. I'm taking up as much space as I can.

We value others, in part, because they store our memories for us. "Remember the time when . . .?" Their minds are extensions of our mind. While they live, part of us lives.

I hired a family friend to draw illustrations of my kids as I remember them. Here they are. Aren't my kids lovely? They are brave and kind and smart as whips. Now that part of me lives in you too.

If you remember my kids the way I remember them, will I live through you?

December 17, 2022

My mother is visiting. She told me that this summer, soon after my diagnosis, seventeen new murals were painted in The Dalles. One reads "H. L. Davis, 1894–1960. American author and poet. Winner of the Pulitzer Prize."

Whaddyaknow?

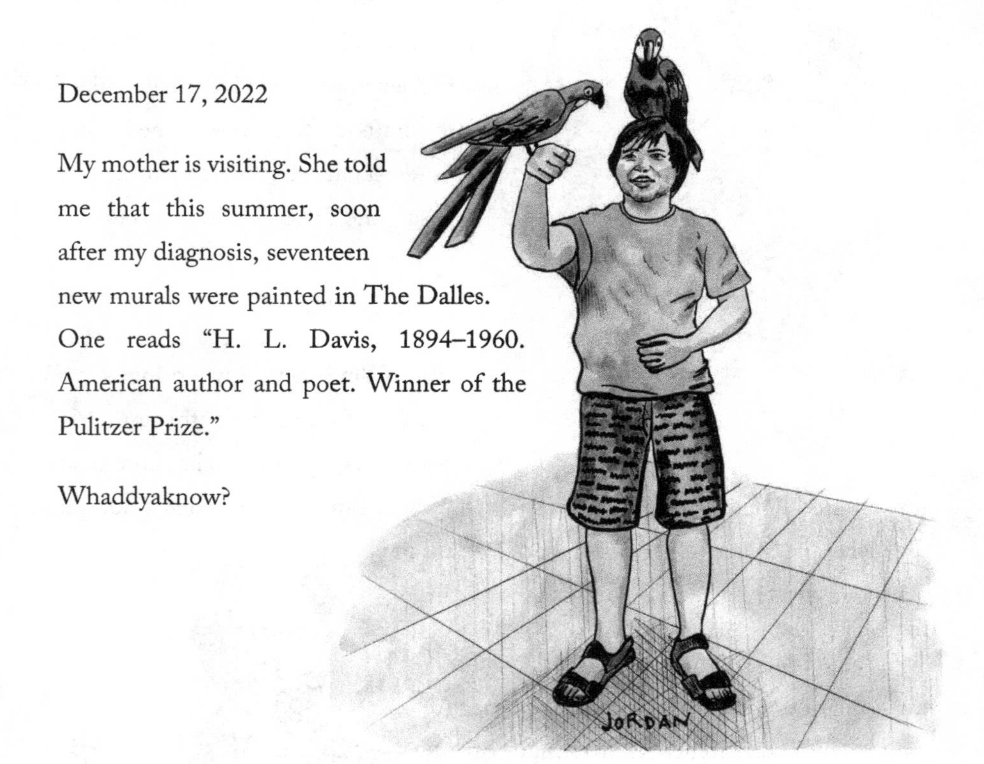

Inspiration 32

Life's greatest joys are found in friends and family. So are life's greatest sorrows.

I have found nothing in life to be more joyful than marriage and children. In third place sharing the podium with spouse and children are friends. Nothing else comes close. In friends and family, we find our audience and performances to applaud. We find service and those to serve. We find love and those we love. We don't need riches to find these joys. No special equipment is needed.

There is risk in seeking joy in friends and family. Only a friend can unfriend. Love may be rejected. Loyalty may be betrayed. Death takes us all.

Loss is the price of joy. Pay that price.

Inspiration 31

Kids are worth it.

Kids are expensive. Kids tie us down. Kids take our time.

Kids are worth it. It's all worth it.

That's Enough

December 25, 2022

Merry Christmas! I just took my last 5-FU chemo pill of the year. Taking those pills twice each day has been the hardest thing I've done. It took some doing to shake that poison into my mouth and force myself to swallow. I'm relieved to be done with that for now. I'll find out in a couple of weeks if it's my last chemo pill, ever. I expect to take one more cycle. It will be nice to have the 5-FU smell gone. I can taste it. It's slightly sour, slightly floral. It tastes of nursing home. My flatulence reeks of it. Poison gas of WWI was said to smell of lilacs.

I once had a firecracker blow up in my hand. Ten minutes later, my fingers still stung. The pain was more annoying than anything else. That's how my hands feel now. Feet too. The stinging woke me up this morning. I suspect my nerve damage is permanent. It's been over a month since my last oxaliplatin infusion. From the papers I read, four out of five oxaliplatin patients with nerve pain reported the pain was still there two-and-a-half years later. Thankfully, the pain isn't nearly as bad as it was. If low-key pain is the worst thing that cancer does to me, I'll have gotten off lucky.

My hand pain reminds me of one of my heroes, Chiune "Sempo" Sugihara. Sugihara was a Japanese diplomat stationed in Lithuania in early WWII. He disobeyed Tokyo's orders by issuing visas to escaping Polish Jews. He wrote transit visas up to twenty hours a day for over a month. Imagine how his hands felt. The foreign ministry summoned Sugihara back to Japan. He drafted travel visas all the way to the Kaunas Railway Station. He threw his last visas out his train window to the crowd. "Please forgive me," he said. "I cannot write anymore. I wish you the best." He saved at least two thousand lives. Every time I think of it, I cry.

My hand pain serves no purpose.

I've also been having back pain. That one scared me. Back pain can be a sign of cancer progressing. Mine wasn't. I just was sitting hunched over at my new desk. My posture is terrible. There is something about keeping my head up that feels it must look conceited. I'm not bothered by my being conceited. Looking conceited, though . . . The worst thing about random symptoms is that everything might signal spreading cancer. Headache? Cancer. Fatigue? Cancer. Lump in my groin? Cancer. I'm having to clear my throat again the way I had to before surgery. Cancer? Dr. Hope said that was nonsense (in nicer words).

I don't know if it is the worry, the chemo, or just immaturity, but I'm snapping at Jen more often. I have to resist turning on the cheat code of "cut me some slack—I have cancer." Physical therapy is teaching me to keep my head up straight. Body positioning can change our emotions. Maybe good posture will give me a better attitude. God help us if good posture gives me more self-confidence.

Friends are reaching out. Some have cancer. Some have family members who died of cancer. Two friends have mothers with cancer now. You'd think I'd know what to say to them. I don't. I know a bit of what not to say. I don't tell them it's all for the best. I don't tell them it's God's plan. I don't try to make it better. I mostly listen. I've learned from those who are more acquainted with anguish than I am. One friend told me that my standing witness to her pain helped. Another friend who's a trauma therapist told me that sometimes we don't need to know the right thing to say. We help if we sit with them in their pain. That's enough.

Inspiration 30

There are no heroes without horrors.

I've known some heroes. Your great-uncle Ron Kast is one. He fought in Vietnam. Read his Silver Star citation. You'll see he earned it. To be a hero, he had to face hard things. All heroes do. Some heroes fight injustice, ignorance, and cruelty. Sometimes heroes get worn down by their horrors. "Why is the world this awful?" they ask. This can happen to you too. When it does, if it does, remember that horrors make heroes.

Inspiration 29

It can always be Christmas.

Does the Christmas season make you happy? Why box up your joy? No matter where we go, it can always be Christmas. We can carry Christmas with us all year as though it's our own private bubble of crisp December air we breathe in and sing out. Helping other people makes us happy. We forget about our problems when we help others solve theirs. Plot ways to help others. Then help. We can treat life as one big "Secret Santa" exchange. Why not? Helping others changes who we are in the stories we tell ourselves about ourselves. Years later, we remember the help we gave. We remember we were the helpers.

Sightseeing

January 8, 2023

Happy New Year!

We're wrapping up a family vacation in France. I've been in France before for work. This is the first time I've gone for pleasure. The trip was a gift from my parents. They are here with us. I think they want to lay down some memories in case I die, they die, whichever. I wasn't set on going. It seemed like a lot of bother, and I didn't want to be thinking, "Is this the last time?" (But what if it is the last time?) It would have made miserable memories for everyone if I had taken a pass. I went along. I did feel free to retreat to the hotel whenever I felt used up. That helped.

My best memory of the trip is of my kids on our first day in Paris. I slept most of the day in the hotel while the rest of the family went to sightsee. (That's not the memory.) Jen's a maximizer. On vacation, sleep is for the return flight. I figured (correctly) she would have the kids running from sight to sight without time to stop for a full meal. The January night was cold and wet. I picked up fresh baguettes on the way to meet Jen and the kids at the Eiffel Tower. They swarmed the bread like pigeons—happy, happy pigeons. That's the memory. There is something primal about seeing your own kids eat.

When we reached the viewing platform, Carissa licked the Eiffel Tower. She licked the metal. I didn't ask.

The next day, we drove west to Omaha Beach. My mother wanted us to feel the sacrifice of the D-Day invasion. We did. It's hard to know a place or time without experiencing the sweep of it. I have been following a Twitter account that posts "live" WWII tweets. The tweets started six years ago with the Nazi invasion of Poland. Over the summer were the atomic bombs and VJ Day. I wanted to feel the length of the war in a way I couldn't get from reading a book. Now I wanted to feel the expanse of the land. As we drove through Normandy, I couldn't help but picture the troops marching through time along the hedgerows: GIs in WWII, doughboys in WWI, Henry V's longbowmen, William the Conqueror's army from the Bayeux Tapestry, Julius Caesar's legions. At the American cemetery, I walked the full length of the field of white crosses and stars of David. I wanted to feel the expanse of that too. Nine thousand lives.

The following day we exhausted ourselves without exhausting the Louvre. I love museums. Even when healthy, I have limits. That place is enormous.

We took the train south to the French Alps. We hiked the steep streets to a historic graveyard set in the ruins of a fortress overlooking the alpine village of Tende. I found it hard to imagine past generations scraping out a living. The farming terraces were narrow and more rock than soil. Each calorie must have counted. I paid more attention to strangers' graves than I normally do. Surely a life cannot be reduced to a name and number. I found myself having the same panic of insignificance I get when trying to scale my mind to the roughly one hundred billion people who have ever lived. I have to flip my thinking and join myself to the whole tapestry to feel magnified by the expanse, not microscopic under it. Future generations will find us unbearably primitive to have allowed our own bodies to kill us through unconstrained cellular growth. Death by cancer will be quaint.

We ended in the South of France, where characters in Victorian novels took in the "healing air." Were those novels set in January? In January, the South of France was all rain. After dinner, Jen and the kids went to the beach to dip their toes into the Mediterranean. Patrick and Carissa brought their bathing suits to do a full polar-bear swim. I walked back to the hotel. As I walked, I realized I hadn't really understood my cancer. I decided to do some sightseeing of my own in online cancer journals.

From my pathology report:

> One of the lymph nodes is positive for metastatic carcinoma with scattered signet ring cells.

Just what is a "signet-ring cell"?

I took my first microbiology class my sophomore year in high school. Microbiology seemed to be as much magic as science. The words would be at home in a spell book: blood agar, chromatic aberration, Erlenmeyer flask, xylene fixation, Gram's crystal violet. That Halloween I dyed my hands purple with the Gram's crystal violet stain I filched from the lab. Gram's crystal violet makes the skin look naturally purple rather than painted. I wore a yellow shirt for contrast. In microbiology class, I learned to embed tissue samples in paraffin, slice off sheets one cell thick—half the thickness of the thinnest membrane of an onion—fix the tissue to a slide, and stain the tissue so cellular landmarks could be seen under a microscope. At first, magnified tissue appears to be a meaningless bunch of blobs. It's like ultrasound or a CT scan in that way. Only the most obvious landmarks have names to the sightseer. What familiar landmarks can you see with a microscope? A chicken egg is a single cell. There is a white. There is a yolk. You will see those on a tissue prep slide. Keep looking. After spending a few minutes exploring the immense world of the small, tissue that is healthy will become familiar to you. You will know normal cells, their shapes, what parts go where.

Signet-ring cancer cells are easy to spot under a microscope. The landmarks are there, just in the wrong shapes, sizes, and places. In a signet-ring cell, the white of the egg has filled with mucus and grown huge. The yolk is squished to one end and flattened. The cell looks like the high school class ring I never bought. The yolk is the gemstone. It's even the blood color of the stone of my never-bought class ring. One look, and you will see that signet-ring cells don't belong. That's cancer. You can see it.

What's under the molecular hood, so to speak, of a signet-ring cell? All cancers have mutated DNA. I don't have most of the common signet-ring cell mutations though—not even in *p53,* the tumor-suppressor gene I studied in the lab of the Famous Man at Princeton. The only mutation I have that's commonly seen in signet-ring cancer is *FGFR2*, the gene for a cell growth signaling protein that makes my cancer more deadly. My cancer is also mutated at four other genes: the insulin receptor substrate gene *IRS2*, a cell-proliferation gene *PDGFRB*, a gene called *SOCS1* involved in immune responses, and the gene for the androgen receptor. Are these other four genes responsible for my cancer? We don't know. Can we do anything about the genes we know have mutated? Perhaps for the androgen receptor. I'll have to ask Dr. Hope about chemical castration, which is what prostate cancer patients must endure to slow down their hormone-dependent cancer cells. The other three mutated genes are just trivia. There aren't drugs that target the proteins that these genes encode. At least not yet.

That's as far as the resolution on our image reveals. We can't see more clearly what my cancer is, or at least I can't.

It rained all day and into the evening here in Nice. Before the kids went to swim in the sea, we told each other our best memories from the trip. Jordan's was also from the Eiffel Tower. He said that, when I showed up that evening with the bread, I wasn't a downer. I had a better attitude than he had expected. That's a lesson for me. I'm glad I broke his expectations.

Carissa

Jordan and my mom have the videos, but I can confirm that I do not regret it at all!

Jen

I accidentally fell into the Mediterranean.

Jessica

lol

Time to pack.

Inspiration 28

Don't spank kids.

I wish I hadn't spanked kids.

There is no evidence spanking works and quite a bit that shows spanking gives kids behavior problems. My other bully's father—the one from church—posts on social media about how his generation spanked their kids and they turned out fine. About that . . .

.

Inspiration 27

Memories matter. Things are just things.

When you have extra money to spend, buy experiences over things. We enjoy the cooking class more than the food processor. The hike matters more to us than the new boots. As I think back on each of you kids, it's the memories that count. I remember playing *Magic: The Gathering* with Jordan and Patrick more than the cards we collected. I think of Aidan and Annelise making their animated short films. I won't ever forget watching Jessica in *Into the Woods* or Carissa's death scene in *Triangle* (that one still chokes me up). I'll always remember being at the top of the World Trade Center with Mallory and at the Vasa Museum with your mother. Things bore us, but we treasure experiences.

¡Viva la Revolución!

January 14, 2023

Jen likes Dr. Hope.

It's my last week of chemo before radiation. I have subtly kept Jen away from Duke Cancer Center until this week. I wanted to keep my doctor discussions on the science side. No sugarcoating. It would be natural if Dr. Hope were to soften things for family members. I waited until the last week of oral chemo to make introductions. I gave Jen a tour of my home away from home. "This is where I get my pager. This is where I get my port jabbed. This is where I get my second pager. The grand piano is on the lower level. We wait here for forty-five minutes. Infusion is on the top level. Yes, the paintings are lovely."

Jen got to ask her questions. Jen liked Dr. Hope's answers. "She thinks the way I do," Jen said. I was also happy to hear some of the answers. "We don't know" is more credible coming from an expert than from someone like me, who is just a motivated amateur who could easily have missed something.

"What caused his cancer? How long has it been growing? Why does chemotherapy cause nerve pain?"

"We don't know. We don't know. We don't know."

I asked Dr. Hope if my mutated androgen receptor gene meant we should try chemical castration, a common treatment for prostate cancer. "No data," she said. Whew. She then told us a cautionary tale about a targeted chemotherapy that worked well on melanoma with a single amino-acid change in a single gene, *BRAF*. The drug should work on any cancer with the same mutation in the same *BRAF* gene, right? They tried. They failed. The drug had no benefit on colorectal cancers with the same mutation in the same gene. That result was surprising. We expect targeted treatment to be logical. We expect cancer mutations to tell us which cancers are alike on the inside, have the same genetic machinery, are treatable with the same drugs. It didn't work that way for *BRAF*-V600E cancers. It's a reason to be cautious with cancer treatments even when everything seems logical. We don't know enough to make our logic logical. Frustrating.

So Dr. Hope's not going to chemically castrate me just because my androgen receptor gene is mutated. To be clear, I was in no way looking forward to chemical castration.

I also got in a question to Dr. Hope expressly to get Jen off my back about my admittedly awful diet. "I'm not saying I'm going to do this," I asked, "but hypothetically, if I started smoking, would this appreciably change my odds of dying from gastric cancer?"

"You want to smoke to lose weight?" Dr. Hope asked.

"I'm not going to start smoking. This is a thought experiment."

Dr. Hope closed her eyes to answer. "No. That wouldn't change your risk. I'd tell you not to do it for general health. But, no, it's not really going to change the numbers."

"Same thing with my diet?" I asked. "If I eat better, will that change my prognosis?"

Her eyes flicked open. She doesn't have to think about this one. I think she's gotten this question before. "No." She shook her head.

Why not? Let's say I didn't have cancer. How much risk would I have if I didn't change my diet? In a whole lifetime, only about one in one hundred men get gastric cancer. Put that 1% risk against my 50% risk of dying from the gastric cancer I already have. And there is no way that changing my diet would get rid of the 1% risk because I have less than half a normal lifespan ahead of me (even if I had no cancer) and because there are so many non-dietary risk factors that lead to gastric cancer.

My takeaway, Jen, is this: Dr. Hope says I can keep eating pecan cookies, pork tamales, and pizza. She's the expert. I'm just the messenger here. Remember you like Dr. Hope. She thinks the way you do.

Dr. Hope finalized her decision to stop my oxaliplatin infusions. My nerve damage is too advanced. I will start radiation in February. Radiation will be daily. Huh? Daily? Radiation seemed like a one-shot thing in *Breaking Bad.* Well, I should say radiation will be daily *except for weekends*. Does cancer take weekends off? I gather radiation oncologists do.

Oh, and I will get to take oral chemotherapy during radiation too. Not that it's a negotiation, but it does feel like "and one more thing" as we're about to shake hands on the deal. Dr. Hope told me to expect even more fatigue during radiation. Friends in the field are telling me the same thing. For the first time, I'm seriously wondering if I will be able to keep up with my work.

Checkout was interminable. I left Jen in the waiting room while I sat in line with five other patients. The wait was so long we got sent to admissions for discharge. It seemed as though we just moved our line from one room to another.

An older patient marched up to the admissions desk to lead a mini-revolt. "We can't wait," she said. She wasn't using her inside voice. "We need our next appointments. Let us back in to the scheduling desk. Buzz us through. Go on. Do it." The poor admissions attendant was overflow for Discharge and trying to help out. I was embarrassed for the patient. "Look at her lording her power over us," the patient said. "She's on a power trip. I'm going to file a complaint, you know." I'm not saying race was a component, but does it surprise you to hear the patient was White and the attendant was not? I don't know if a racial component was inflaming the patient, but I wouldn't blame the attendant for assuming so. "I'm going back in there," the patient announced. "You can't stop me." She caught the door when another patient came out. "Follow me, everyone! What can they do to us? Nothing," she told the other patients in line.

I stayed and apologized to the attendant. "You didn't deserve that," I told her. "What you don't know is what that patient told the rest of us when we were waiting in the back. She has pancreatic cancer. Her husband has esophageal cancer. I think every day may be a bad day for her."

The attendant maintained a professional demeanor. Maybe she knows cancer patients are going through a lot. Maybe she's seen worse. Just another Thursday?

As I left with the important half of my scheduling done (it really was taking a while), the patient burst, triumphant, from Discharge. "Some days you're the villain, and some days you get to be the hero," she told me as she passed. "I got to be a hero today."

I'm writing this in my local pizza joint. A little girl is dancing to a song only she can hear. I think she's doing it to make her shoes light up. It's delightful. Last Saturday in France, I also saw a kid dancing in a restaurant. That restaurant served North African cuisine, far from the tourist strip. The kid danced back and forth on the restaurant bench with no relation I could see to the North African music. My second-best memory from France—after that of my kids eating baguettes—is that boy dancing up and down the restaurant booth while his parents carried on. They had eyes only for each other. As I think back on it, I've seen the essence of this dance before. It's the dance only a child will do, perhaps only a child *can* do. The dance reminded me of Aidan, who—completely out of character as I know him—entered an elementary school talent show. Aidan was going to dance to music from the Disney film *Happy Feet*. I had never known Aidan to dance. I thought, *I wonder how this going to go?* How it went was show-stopping. Just like the penguin in the movie, Aidan danced with abandon. His feet moved faster than I've ever seen them move. On and on he danced, his untrained feet flying. Aidan has an enormous head—just ask Jen about birthing him—and his wide face was filled to the edges with one of those smiles that pulls back the eyebrows and seems to shine out. It's the most joy I have ever seen pour from one person. Aidan kept it up all the way through the cheers.

I miss having young children in the house.

It didn't take long for oral chemo to kick in after my appointment. I had alternating chills and hot flashes through the night. Menopausal women everywhere are nodding knowingly. I guess it's a final "eff you" from the oral 5-FU.

I know my prognosis has not changed, but I'm feeling the push to get everything done that I want to get done. I don't know if it's a premonition. I don't know if it's a warning from a kindly Father in Heaven. Maybe it's just depression or the pizza I ate—"more of gravy than of grave," as Ebenezer Scrooge put it. Whatever the source, I feel the imperative. I must work while I can. If my condition worsens, I will want everything off my plate other than family. Time is ticking down. Am I hearing the Final Jeopardy music playing?

I tried calling my ninety-two-year-old friend, Sam the Statistician. We have been talking each week since he heard I had cancer. No answer. Bit concerning.

Next week, Dr. Hope will attend the world's most important gastrointestinal cancer conference. The United States is at the forefront of most cancer research. The exception is gastric cancer. Gastric cancer is less common in the US. The center of the gastric cancer universe lies somewhere over the Sea of Japan. South Korea, Japan, and China are the research leaders. That's where the patients are. The conference is in San Francisco, where the gastric oncologists will meet in person for the first time since Covid. If there is something new for my cancer, we'll read about it next week.

Inspiration 26

Gift attention to your spouse.

A relationship that lasts is built on attention. When your spouse says something, respond. It doesn't matter if you think it's silly. Let your spouse know you heard. A "meaningless" point from a spouse isn't meaningless any more than an "accidental" touch when you were dating was an accident. What is the meaning of a spouse's random question? John Gottman calls it a "bid for attention." The question under the question is a simple one: "Do you still care about me?" Answer that question with a *yes*.

When a spouse asks you to join an activity, don't judge just based on what you want to do. A spouse asking for your participation is like a dancer leaping across the stage. Catch if you can.

I learned this late. I let your mom do a lot of things alone because I thought the activities sounded boring. I'm trying to do better.

Inspiration 25

Treat others as if they are going through the hardest time in their life.

You'd be surprised what some people are going through. They may look happy. They may seem to have it all figured out. The surface you see could be the paint on a house gutted by fire. What you aren't seeing could be a scene of suffering: the parents whose adopted child smashed their grand piano; the couple in the eleventh month of secret separation; the mother who miscarried and decided she had to pretend that nothing had happened; the classmate whose earliest memory was of being molested; the man who lost his wife, his kids, his house, his career, and his parents in the same year. These are all people I know. You'd never guess by looking at them. I didn't.

Like *Shark Tank*

Bearded son-in-law: *Then you started regular work?*

After business school, I got a job as a tech-transfer executive at Los Alamos and then joined a biotech spin-out. After the biotech spin-out, I started consulting for pharma.

I got my pharma consulting job just before the housing bubble collapsed into the Great Recession. The job was across the country in North Carolina. The family wanted to stay in Los Alamos for the school year. I left to work at a distance. I came back on some weekends. I'd get on an afternoon flight on a Friday in Philadelphia, land in Albuquerque late evening, and be in Los Alamos by 1:00 A.M. I'd have to leave the family eighteen hours later. That was not for me. I learned from leaving them just how much I needed my family. When I was away from them, my world seemed to shrink. I got small along with my small world. I don't think it was good for Jen or the kids either. But we needed the job. I was glad to have it.

I was excited to work as a consultant. My company sold projects based on my rNPV equation. I told them right away, as a rookie consultant, "I invented rNPV. Did you know that?" They weren't interested. But it was freaking true. In fact, they acted as if I'd passed gas. I know, now, that I had seemed completely full of myself. Former managers told me that was my reputation. Worse, any rookie consultant knows basically nothing about pharma. It's just too hard a field to know until you are in it. I'd say annoying things about how important rNPV was while messing up the lingo in ways that exposed how little I knew. I'm lucky they didn't fire me.

As hard as Princeton was, as hard as business school was, consulting was harder. The hours were longer. The learning curve was steeper. The stakes were higher. It was the perfect job for me.

I got to work with pharma clients all over the world. I got a crack at solving their biggest problems. These problems came so quickly that I didn't have time to procrastinate. It was the opposite of the endless nature of lab work that I had found so depressing at Princeton. There was no time to ruminate. Every day, I woke up thinking about client problems. I had no time to think about my own problems.

After I really learned to be a consultant, I was promoted to running mergers and acquisitions diligence for our parent company. I did the diligence work for the pharma deals that smaller companies brought to ours for investment. These were real pharma drugs, and we had real money to invest. Most deals that crossed my desk didn't make a lick of sense. You've heard of a *yes* man? I was the *no* man. My boss got me an electronic *No!* button. I was paid to say *no* a lot.

Like the show Shark Tank?

I was the *Shark Tank* guy. I did that for a year. We changed CEOs, and the company didn't want to do those kinds of deals. I returned to consulting. We merged and became a huge publicly traded company. I started leading consulting teams. It's what I do today.

Leading a team is its own skill set. Doing the work is one thing. Getting other people to do the work is different. It's a hard transition. You have to learn how to give people under you the chance to succeed, which means they might fail. You have to encourage and mentor. It's almost like raising kids. You start out by doing things for them. But they have to learn to do things themselves.

I decided to focus on pricing and market access. Pharma companies need to get an insurance company to cover their drugs. This usually means pharma companies have to drive a pile of money up to insurance companies in the form of a rebate. The number one cost for almost any branded retail drug—the pills you pick up at your local CVS or Walgreens—is the rebate that pharma has to pay insurance companies to put the drug on formulary so you and I can get the drug covered. That rebate regularly exceeds a third of the entire price of the drug. We describe it as being like Jos. A. Bank: buy two, get one free (for the insurance company). In competitive drug classes, the rebate is "buy one, get one free." Understanding how to negotiate that rebate—what rebate to pay and why—that's what I do now.

It turns out that consulting-wise, drug pricing and market access are a lot easier to sell than rNPV. Here's an example. I had a client in a small company called CoLucid. My team did the forecast and the rNPV for their migraine drug. We helped them with merger negotiations. CoLucid sold for $960 million. You know what additional work I got from CoLucid? Nothing. I never had them as a client again. They were sold.

You're gone as a consultant.

The best I could do was to try to track the C-suite down at their next company and say, "Remember that good work I did for you?" In contrast, in market access, doing a good job means more work from a successful client, not less work from a client that no longer exists because it was bought.

I also do copay assistance optimization. I just love that work because it justifies pharma companies paying for patient copays. It's the best deal in pharma. Pharma will pay for a patient's entire deductible if the economics are right. I design those programs now. I love helping scientists, inventors, and clinicians get their inventions to be commercial successes. With copay assistance, I also get to help patients pay for their drugs. It's satisfying.

So that gets me to now. Our last child, Annelise, was born here in North Carolina. She's number seven. They are all great kids. I just can't say enough about my kids. They're just good people.

I've known your kids for about five years now. They are good people.

I haven't talked much about what raising kids was like. Jordan was the first one, and the first one is hard. The lack of sleep just about did me in. That's the hard part. Kids take a lot of work, and at the beginning you know nothing. I tell new parents two children aren't as hard as two of the first. When you've grown your own babysitters, then it's all good.

I love watching kids learn. They learn so fast. I got to help teach mine to talk and crawl and roll over. I still can recite Dr. Seuss from memory. I got to read books with all the character voices. Harry Potter was great for that. I got to introduce to them my favorite childhood books. I taught them science and math and history and trivia. I loved every bit of that. Some of them pursued acting. Carissa is serious about it. I love acting, and it's a thrill to see them do it better than I did. I love music, and Mallory plays the trumpet far better than I ever did. Patrick sang in the Santa Fe Opera. Jordan is deeper into math and physics than I am. Jessica knows more about film than I do. Aidan is better at computers than I am. Annelise is young, but she already uses technology better than I do. As they've gotten to be young adults, it's been a joy to see them choose kindness. They are kind kids, all of them. I enjoy seeing them go beyond me. They teach me now. I love that.

That's my life until now with the exception of cancer.

Inspiration 24

If it doesn't pay, it's not a job. It's a hobby.

The world may not pay for our hobbies. If it doesn't pay, it's not a job. Don't get me wrong. Most of us want more than a paycheck out of a job. It's a bonanza when pay comes with friends, purpose, and personal growth. The best jobs bring us all those things. The best jobs yoke our talents to our passions. But the best jobs also pay us. The world wants something from us, and it tells us what it wants by paying us. Pay is the language it speaks. Everything but pay we can find elsewhere if we must. We can volunteer on weekends. We can listen to music while driving. We can write at night. A job doesn't have to be everything. A job does have to pay.

Inspiration 23

You will get your good jobs through personal connections.

How can this be? Most jobs are with companies, and big companies follow a structured hiring process. These companies cast a wide net to find the best applicants. That's the problem. A large applicant pool means your own odds of getting that job approach zero. When you have a personal connection, the applicant pool can narrow to one person: you. A personal connection solves your large-pool problem. Even if many more jobs in the world are filled through structured searches, the good jobs you end up getting will most likely come through your personal connections. The odds are better. A friend can alert you to an upcoming job opening, before there is a structured search. Your personal connection may build the job requirements around your experience. When you look back on your career, you will (probably) find that personal connections worked and resumé blasts didn't.

Gifts

January 29, 2023

My fifty-first birthday was Friday. All the kids came, even Mallory, who took the train home from college. At the party, Carissa came out and said it: "We should have fun. It could be your last birthday." Yes, it might be my last birthday. Let's make the most of it. I'm glad she said it. It kept me from carrying the weight of maintaining appearances.

We had a lovely evening of pizza, cheesecake, and *Trivia Murder Party*. Jen skunked us with perfect play. We call Jen "the strongest link" now. She'll appear on the game show *The Weakest Link* sometime this year. We're still sworn to silence on how she did, but her new nickname should tell you that she was at least pleased with her performance. She was radiant when she returned from taping in L.A. I'm so happy for her. Jen also was on *Jeopardy!* during our Princeton days. Her knowledge base was fantastic—better than mine, at least—but her buzzer timing was abysmal. Her losing on *Jeopardy!* was a disappointment to her, you might say. She threw a tub of butter substitute at the hotel wall. The fake butter splattered across the room. The front desk told us to keep it down or we'd be asked to leave. I enjoy calling her "the strongest link." I enjoy her reaction. She perks up. She really is the strongest link. I'm glad when other people see it too.

The morning before my birthday, I took my last pre-radiation 5-FU pills. I'm feeling physically the best I have since chemo started. No more chills. I'm walking with nearly my old stamina. I still have the peripheral neuropathy, the hand and foot pain. It still wakes me up some nights, but it's not as bad as it was.

The international gastrointestinal cancer conference results are out. Dr. Hope attended. As a gift to myself, I read the published abstracts from the talks and poster sessions. Scientists communicate in unusual ways sometimes. A conference poster session is one of those ways. Medical conferences have rooms filled with posters twice the size of those at movie theaters. The conference posters are tacked to row after row of portable poster stands. Research study authors hang out by each poster to answer questions. It's like a child's science fair but with none of the hand-drawn monarch butterflies. These posters are high-quality, laminated, and filled with tiny text and Kaplan-Meier cancer-survival curves. Look for crowds to know which posters are reporting breakthroughs.

From my bedroom in North Carolina, I couldn't see the crowds clustering around the posters in San Francisco. I just had the words. There were 202 abstracts in the gastrointestinal category. I had to find the ones that were relevant to me. Gastric cancer or gastro-esophageal-junction cancer: check. Adenocarcinoma: check. Vaccine for a HER2-positive cancer that my tumor doesn't express: no good, whomp-whomp. Immunotherapy that targets the PD-1 system my cancer doesn't make: also, whomp-whomp. FGFR2 that my cancer overproduces: check. And so on.

Most posters boiled down to "this chemotherapy gave patients a few weeks more to live." The closest thing I could find to a game changer was called claudin 18.2. Claudins are new to me. They were discovered in 1998 and did not appear in any of my Princeton coursework. The drug that targets claudin was developed by a German biotech that was acquired by a Japanese large-pharma. Neither has been my client. Claudins are proteins that hook cells together. It turns out that gastric cancers can make a lot of one type of claudin, claudin 18.2. When scientists see a cancer producing a lot of one protein, they say with satisfaction, "Gotcha." An over-producing protein is a target. A new target means a new drug. And a new drug can mean new life.

A new druggable target is a big deal.

From my reading, the best results for gastric cancer were from the phase III trial of a drug that targets claudin 18.2. Clinical trials are branded these days with cool-sounding names that are often tortured acronyms. The SPOTLIGHT trial tested a claudin 18.2-targeting drug called zolbetuximab. Without the new drug targeting claudin 18.2, 63% of patients died during the trial. With the new drug, only 53% of patients died. Nearly all patients had nausea. Vomiting risk was doubled with the drug. But for another 10% chance at a longer life? I'd take it.

I'd like to hear what my friend Sam the Statistician thinks. He designs cancer clinical trials. He hasn't responded to texts or emails. It's been a month. Since he's ninety-two, I think I'm right to be concerned. I pinged his work. No response. Nothing is in the Philadelphia obituaries.

But does my cancer make lots of claudin 18.2? If my cancer doesn't, the drug will be useless for me. I checked my next-generation DNA sequencing. Claudin 18.2 was not listed. I emailed the DNA-testing company. They do not test for claudin 18.2. The target's too new and is probably protected by patents. So we wait.

I asked Dr. Hope if she had the same reaction as I had to the conference. She did. She said she expects FDA approval for zolbetuximab for claudin 18.2-positive gastric adenocarcinoma. So do I. If this were a client project, I'd expect the drug to be approved next year. Will that be in time for me?

For my birthday, Carissa picked me out a hat. It's a cancer-patient-turned-drug-lord Heisenberg hat from *Breaking Bad*. Too funny. I look like a gunslinger but also a bit ridiculous. I don't really do scary.

I get my next CT scan in three days. I'm nervous. It's the first scan since chemotherapy. The best thing we could see would be nothing.

Inspiration 22

Reading time buys screen time.

I think our single best parental invention was the reading/screen-time bank. To earn screen time, Jordan and Patrick had to read. Reading time was their currency. If they had read, we didn't care that the time was spent on television or video games. The older kids read reams while learning through experience about earning, saving, and spending. The time bank was a brain lever and an economics lesson in one package. The system worked so long as we policed it. The time sheet requires consistent, harsh policing so it's less tempting to cheat.

I wish we had kept up the time sheet for all you kids. I'm sad to say I coasted with you younger kids. These days we'd probably add in exercise time, maybe even at a double rate. We raised smart but too often sedentary kids.

Inspiration 21

A solvable problem is a gift.

Take joy in solving problems. Notice when you do get a problem that's solvable and you solve it. Too many problems are chores without permanent solutions. We can feel as though we are living in a mud hut. Every night the walls slump in. Every day we push the mud back into place. You'll find that raising kids can be a long slog of chores, not a set of problems you solve. Chores are a drag. If you can turn your chores into mini-problems you solve, do that. It feels better. You can even say *ding* as though you leveled up in a video game. Keep an eye on chores versus solvable problems when you are parents. The parent with more chores may need fewer of those and more problems to solve. Doing chores and solving problems may both count as "work," but they aren't the same.

Hold Your Breath

February 1, 2023

"Breathe in!" the CT scanner orders me.

The CT scanner uses a recorded male voice. "Breathe in" is not a request. CT scanner doesn't ask. CT scanner tells. CT scanner tolerates no funny business. My sixth-grade teacher in The Dalles used the same tone with me. He was not amused.

I breathe in. I have built my lung capacity over years of singing on stage and in choirs. I know how to breathe the efficient way: deep down with my diaphragm. I keep my shoulders still. I relax my neck and face. I breathe in to fill myself to the small of my back. Strength in speech comes from the deep places.

"Hold your breath!"

Today is my first CT scan since chemotherapy. This one is a big one. There are two possible outcomes: no news and the worst news. Nothing good can come of this. I have been worrying about this CT scan even though I don't expect we will see more tumors. New tumors would have had to thrive despite chemotherapy. I figured that could happen only if—and Dr. Hope confirmed my thinking—my cancer were maximally aggressive, maximally lethal.

Microscopic cancer can't be spotted by a CT scan. The smallest tumors a CT scan can see are about the size of the BBs I used to shoot on my family's farm when I was a child. The thought of BBs draws me into memory.

As much as I loved my childhood BB gun—and I did love it—I can't remember anything living I hit that really made me proud. The closest thing to an amusing living target was a huge crow, which I shot as it perched in a cherry tree. I remember it because I was with a companion, probably my cousin Gary. The crow was too big to be hurt greatly by our BBs. It squawked in confusion as we each hit the bird several times from our cover behind the barn fence. The crow flew off in, I thought at the time, indignation. Crows are the smartest birds. I didn't think about that then. Everything else living I hit—grasshoppers, lizards, small birds—gave me little pleasure. I was proud of my aim, but what I felt whenever I went to admire my handiwork was emptiness.

One summer my father confiscated my BB gun. I deserved it. I had hiked to the top of our hill with my sister Amy and her friend Jami. I took my BB gun along, probably to seem manly. The view from the top of our hill is stunning. One can see Mt. Hood—a picture-postcard mountain that so perfectly looks the way a mountain should look that it doesn't seem possible. To the north, many miles of the Columbia River carve an enormous letter *Z* with an elongated base. When I was in the third grade, I thought the Columbia looked like the *Z* on my Zips tennis shoes. I made the hike often to stand on top of my world and take it in.

When I visit the top of the hill now, I can't help but measure with my eye where the Missoula floods are said to have reached in the last Ice Age. Starting about fifteen thousand years ago, a temporary lake called Lake Missoula formed repeatedly in Montana, four hundred miles to the northeast. Lake Missoula filled with glacial runoff bounded by walls of ice. Each fifty years—my lifetime, depending—Lake Missoula filled to hold as much water as lakes Erie and Ontario combined. The lake would become so full that the water pressure itself was great enough to melt the base of the ice dams that held the water back. Downriver lies The Dalles.

When the ice dams broke, Lake Missoula was emptied of all its water in a few days. There is only one way for the water to go to reach the sea: the narrow Columbia River Gorge. My sister Amy is a state trooper detective in Oregon now. If she had been patrolling I-84 at the end of the Ice Age, her radar gun could have clocked the floodwater rushing past at eighty miles per hour. If my math is correct, the floodwaters filled the entire gorge. Our hill became an island in the torrent. This happened at least seventy and perhaps one hundred times in a row. When the floods were the highest, every thousand years or so, our hill was engulfed by three hundred feet of water and mud. Anyone unfortunate enough to have settled in The Dalles was wiped from history. The water swallowed up our hill and dumped sand and a granite boulder from who-knows-where on top. Fifteen thousand years later, that sand lies at the crest of our hill above the native bedrock and beneath the dry grass and scrub oak.

Jami wore tight designer jeans on our hike to the top of the hill. I don't know how much work it takes to slip into jeans that tight, but Jami had put in the effort. She had the big hair of the 1980s with "mile-high bangs" (her words). Her lips shone with the balm that came in a brass tin with a sliding lid. All the cool girls had one. Jami came from the part of town with the nice houses. I thought she was a little bit stuck up. At one point as we climbed our hill, Jami bent over in front of me. I can't recall why she bent over. To look more closely into a hole in case a snake was inside? What I recall clearly as I lie on the CT scanner following orders is the sight of Jami's buttocks in her too-tight jeans presenting themselves to me as a perfect target.

I don't know why I did it. In one impulsive motion, I lifted my BB gun and shot Jami in the behind. I felt awful. I felt awful immediately and not only because I knew I would get in trouble (as I did). I couldn't believe I had acted on impulse.

I have seldom been impulsive before or since.

I didn't find where my dad hid my BB gun until I returned home from college as a married man.

In the CT scanner, it would be a poor time to laugh. I hold my breath and lie as still as I can. The CT scanner is a doughnut that is taller than I am. I had lain down on the scanner table and dropped my jeans to keep the metal zipper and belt buckle from blocking the X-rays. I hold still when ordered not because the voice of command cows me but because I want the scan to be clear and any BB-sized tumors visible. The X-ray source whirls in the doughnut about me. The table where I lie extracts me slowly from the doughnut. The X-rays scan me from collarbone to pelvis. In six seconds, I receive a year's worth of radiation.

"Breathe," says the CT scanner. The recording is less demanding this time. Perhaps the voice actor knew we wouldn't need an order to breathe. We need only permission.

Inspiration: from the Latin *inspirare,* meaning "to breathe."

My favorite character in my favorite book as a child was the wizard Gandalf. I loved the thought of being full of arcane knowledge, otherworldly, above. It wasn't until I was an adult that I appreciated Gandalf's greatest power is not his fire magic. Gandalf's deepest strength is his gift of inspiring others. Gandalf encourages all—from hobbits to kings—to fight evil, to face the hard thing, to be their best selves. As I have grown in years, I have circled back to my childhood idol to identify again with Gandalf, at least in my hopes. I find joy in the cultivation of consultants and children. I take satisfaction, though the task can wear me down, in drawing out disinformation that has spread like a cancer through too many adults I care about—some of whom I admire, some of whom I pity. I try to be patient. It can take years to cleanse tumorous lies from the mind of a friend.

We're taught to think of erosion as a gradual process on a geologic timeframe. We learn that mountains become plains through the weathering of wind and the slow drip, drip of rain, year after year. More often, change is slow until it's not. The pressure builds slowly. The change comes in a flood that reshapes the land.

During Covid, I reconnected with Jami over social media. I sent my friend request with "I'm sorry I shot you in the butt." She laughed and was gracious. She was, it turns out, not a little bit stuck up as a child but a little bit shy. I didn't know. She's grown to become a woman of integrity and influence. She is raising a lovely family in Montana—in the spot, in fact, where Lake Missoula formed and flooded. It's delightful to see people grow. It's humbling to realize I had misjudged her.

"Breathe in! Hold your breath! Breathe." The CT scanner swallows me up and spits me out three times.

On my third pass through the CT scanner, my nurse injects a contrast dye through my port. The dye is used to block X-rays, and this makes some blood vessels easy to see. The dye briefly makes me feel flushed. The scan tech had warned me beforehand that the dye could make me feel as though I had wet myself. I don't know about that. Does wetting yourself burn? The dye burns the back of my throat and my groin. The contrast dye is nephrotoxic—it harms kidneys—but that's the least of my concerns at the moment.

I got my test results later that evening while driving with Aidan to visit Jessica. We were driving to Jessica's apartment because she had called with an emergency. She had tried to reframe a finished puzzle of fighting dragons. This puzzle was first finished by Layne, my bearded son-in-law, and his grandmother. His grandmother died of cancer when Layne was young. She had framed the finished puzzle for Layne to remember her by. While I was getting my CT scan, Jessica attempted to move the puzzle from one picture frame to a new one as a surprise for Layne. Jessica dropped the puzzle. She spent the next four hours trying to get all the pieces back in place before Layne returned from work. She was only halfway done and wasn't going to make it. So she called in an emergency puzzle-solving team. That's Aidan and me. I wore my *Breaking Bad* hat.

I had my phone read the CT scan results to me as I drove.

Findings:

- Liver: Normal in morphology and enhancement. No suspicious hepatic masses are identified.
- Kidneys: No suspicious renal lesions.
- Gastrointestinal Tract: No abnormal dilation or wall thickening.
- Lymph Nodes: No retroperitoneal or mesenteric lymphadenopathy.

Impression:

No evidence of recurrent or metastatic disease.

No evidence of recurrent or metastatic disease. I listened to that twice. What a relief. I'm not completely clear, but this is an important hurdle. I will need two years of negative results after radiation is done to know this cancer will not kill me.

Layne returned home ten minutes before we could finish the puzzle. Jessica had tried to delay him by wheedling for Chinese food in the most suspicious, guilty tone possible. She followed with unconvincing reasons that he—and not she—needed to pick up said Chinese food. Layne is a smart man, and he knows Jessica well. He knew something was up the whole time. He entered the apartment to find the three of us on the carpet putting the last pieces in place.

I hope Layne sees the goodness in Jessica more than he sees the accident. He knows she didn't mean anything but good, but it can be hard to be understanding sometimes when our actions touch on the death of those we love.

The last few days the pressure had built in me over this CT scan. Even though I know the end can come rapidly any time—at least until I'm really in the clear—I am far from ready to go. This night, at least, the dam continues to hold back the flood. I can breathe again.

No word, still, from Sam the Statistician. I was able to get in contact with Michele, a friend from Martin's lab at Princeton. She also coauthored papers with Sam. The last time Sam and I talked, he had mentioned Michele and how much we both liked and respected her. Sam told me a story about how Michele had taken Sam aside and given him—a much older married man—a piece of her mind about his hitting up a younger visiting researcher. Michele didn't realize the younger visiting researcher was, in fact, Perry, Sam's wife. Sam and I had a laugh over that. Michele hasn't heard from Sam either. She gave me Martin's phone number. Perhaps he has heard from Sam.

Inspiration 20

Be your toddler's life narrator.

I think it's a wise choice for parents to talk to their toddlers *all the time*. "You are walking. Walking, walking, walking." "Daddy's washing the dishes. Wash, wash, wash." "Changing your diaper. There we go, clean." We become our child's soundtrack narration. I think narrating our kids' lives does more than help them learn language. I think the narration helps our kids make sense of the world.

Inspiration 19

When you keep falling down the same cliff, seek a different way up.

Some life problems we keep failing. We find ourselves trying to climb the same cliff, only to fall and fall and fall. We may feel weak. We may feel worthless. We may feel we are broken. We aren't. What may be true is that we can't climb this cliff with the tools we have. We may need climbing ropes. We may need a friend to belay our line. We may need to grow another inch before we can reach the last fingerhold. Walk away from the cliff. Let the problem go for a time. Do something else. Come back another season. You may even spot a better route up.

Sad in a Dumb Way

My bearded son-in-law, Layne: *I was just thinking about the coronavirus stuff. I don't know if you're going to go into that.*

Sure. I started watching Covid in December of 2019. I was watching it because my work at Los Alamos was on the mathematics of viruses. I'm not an expert anymore, but I used to be.

It's your territory.

It's my territory. I can't say I'm a professional. These days, I say I'm a strong amateur. I also had a colleague whose parents lived in Wuhan. My colleague and I were both alarmed by the early reports. Once we saw what's called the R_0, the basic reproductive number of the virus, we knew it could get bad unless the virus were stopped right there in Wuhan. R_0 tells you how many people each person will infect. The R_0 was high. "Oh, that's bad," I thought. "That's really bad." It's like how a seismologist sees lines on a graph and knows there was an earthquake halfway across the ocean and a tsunami is coming.

I worked on virus epidemiology models while I was at Los Alamos. I don't have an epi model set up now, but I've developed an intuitive sense of how these models work. I couldn't calculate how bad it was going to be, but I knew it was going to be bad. I started warning people in January. Jen said I sounded kind of nutty. [1]

It didn't take long until a bunch of complete frauds started convincing people that Covid was no big deal. This included some economists and some super-sketchy physicians. Politicians started making it a political thing. To cling to one's political identity required some to believe that the coronavirus was just the flu and that everything should open up.

Then the virus was here. I knew from my training that Covid was going to be bad. People were being sent home from work. Everything was shutting down. What

---

[1]This is what I posted January 21, 2020, on Facebook.

> Not good. We don't know how bad it will be, but this is not good. When I look at this as someone who used to study virus transmission, I think:
>
> - It's early
> - It's bad that it goes from person to person
> - It's bad that healthcare workers got it
> - China found the SARS experience to be a threat to the party order, so hopefully they will be ready this time to do better (they are clamping down on social media, so the situation could be worse than the headlines)
> - Once a virus is living well in people, it can evolve
> - It's an RNA virus, so it evolves faster than others (RNA replication is error prone)
> - But it doesn't look like 1918 flu or something, so there is that
> - Chinese New Year is the largest human migration

The CDC confirmed that same day that Covid reached the US. Ten weeks later, Covid hit New York City hard.

could I do? Seriously, what could I do other than keep warning people? I had a computer. I had a phone.

The most immediate problem was the ventilator shortage. More ventilators were being manufactured, but they wouldn't be ready until the summer. There was a limited supply. We were going to run out. The states were all fighting each other for ventilators because, of course, the federal government was making states fight each other. It was stupid.

I woke up with what I thought was a bright idea. "Hey, I have a CPAP machine. I wonder if I could turn a CPAP machine into a ventilator?" I had the CPAP to stop my sleep apnea and snoring. You cannot turn a CPAP machine into a ventilator. That is actually a bad idea. But by asking around, I found a pulmonologist who had the good idea to use something called a BiPAP machine. A BiPAP is like a hospital-grade CPAP machine and is a mini ventilator. It turned out there were a lot of BiPAP machines out there. They are in every hospital, but we don't normally use them as ventilators. My pulmonologist colleague had already used one of these BiPAP machines as a ventilator when his hospital had run out. I started pushing the idea to people in my company who could get things done. This included two former army officers—a retired colonel and a general—who were high up in the company. We got the blessing from our CEO. The retired army brass, the pulmonologist, and I formed a core team to solve the ventilator problem.

We got a huge company group spooled up, probably sixty people. The pulmonologist and I wrote a paper on how to use the BiPAP machines as ventilators. We made training videos. We recorded a podcast. We did all sorts of marketing to doctors and nurses. We ran virtual training sessions. New York and North Carolina quietly bought thousands of BiPAPs. New York's Northwell hospital system ended up collaborating with us on the training. We were in discussions with Vice President Pence's staff on getting the BiPAP training out to hospitals nationwide, but that went cold. We didn't know why at the time. It seemed like the perfect answer and would cost the government nothing. We were training for free. Many hospitals already had the BiPAPs. There was reporting later that Vice President Pence and the president's son-in-law Jared Kushner had a power struggle over who was running the Covid response.

I would find myself bursting out in laughter at the absurdity of trying to save the world from my bedroom. That exaggerates what we accomplished, but that's what it felt like at the time.

Then the wave came. It was that close. And I mean *that* close. When you don't have a ventilator for someone seriously ill with Covid, the patient dies. The last-ditch option is to split a ventilator and use one machine for two patients. You take one ventilator and run two hoses off it and then have two patients breathe at the same time. This is not good for the patients.

It doesn't sound good.

Do you know how many ventilators they had to split in New York City? Two. Only two. New York had the BiPAPs, and with those BiPAPs the city had just enough ventilators.

It's stuff you read about or you see in movies.

It was so close. So close. People don't realize how close it was. But that's how close it was. It was right to the edge in New York City.

The wave came, and then it was time to wait for the vaccines. I volunteered for the Pfizer clinical trial. I thought it would be great to help the science along, but I also wanted to get vaccinated early.

When the vaccines were authorized—which happened much more quickly than I had expected—there were just so many lies told. Deadly lies. I found myself on social media undoing lies about Covid and the vaccines. I hope it helped. I did get messages from people who told me they got vaccinated because of what I posted. If nothing else, I gave other people the words they could use with their own families.

With my parents, I had to tell them too. At first, they didn't want to get vaccinated. They're like, "We're healthy." And I'm like, "It's not about health necessarily." They eventually got their shots.

I'm glad.

I don't know how much I changed their minds, but they still did it, which is good. It's a very, very crazy thing, but I remember you, at a certain point, wanted to get on the Joe Rogan podcast.

We tried. We actually got Rogan's cell number and pitched him on the BiPAPs. We did get our pulmonologist on former governor George Pataki's radio show in New York.

I listen to Rogan, and I like the guy, but he's kind of, I guess for lack of a better term, dumb. He's smart in his way, but he's not the smartest guy, let's say. And he had on a lot of people who were, as you said, pushing a lot of things that even I knew "That doesn't sound right. That doesn't make sense."

They weren't just little lies they told. They told lies that tricked people into a gruesome death by suffocation. I don't know if there is a God. If there is—

That's going to come back.

That's going to be a hard, hard conversation. I think it will be a hard realization for the liars to face what they did. My cousin's cousin believed those lies. Her husband ended up in the hospital. Her father ended up in the hospital. Her brother was in the ICU twice. The first time he was in a coma. She ended up in the ICU and was so sick that she had to be flown to the Mayo Clinic. She had to have her blood removed from her body and put through a heart-lung machine because her lungs were wrecked by Covid. She was there for fifty-four days. She's younger than I am.

People from my hometown, friends of the family, church people would tell me off on Facebook. I have some of these saved to remind myself just how crazy it was.

> I wouldn't get the vaxx if you just handed me the million...seriously!

> Will it keep me from getting Covid? Nope. Do we know exactly the long term or even short term effects? Nope...why is it again I want this?

> Mark my words Jeff...before this is all said and done you and many others will really be wishing you had taken a different approach and hadn't trusted those you did....this is not an argument it is my stand...it is not moveable it will not waver...I'm right and I know it...and I am an excellent judge of character....

> You must actually be part of the deception...that's actually worst...you seem to be the part that sounds like a duck....

> Think what you want Jeff....I'm right you are not...my horse is going to win and yours is gonna break his leg and have to be put down...I know you are very intelligent but you lack in discernment and wisdom...I am sorry for you...I really am...I think the truth will be very painful for you...

> For those of you seeing this conversation...DO NOT GET THE VAXX...DO NOT LISTEN TO THE MEDIA AND THOSE THEY CONTROL...WHICH UNFORTUNATELY INCLUDES THE PERSON I AM TALKING WITH

That guy got Covid. He nearly died. I hear he's in constant pain now. He may never walk right. I wish I had found the right words to help him.

That's what these liars did. They got to my friends. They got to my own extended family. It's horrible. I mean we're at over a million American lives that are just gone.

I can't imagine it, being in your shoes. How frustrating that must have been. I worked with a guy. He's a super nice guy, but every time I bring up vaccines, he's always like, "Oh, no, no. I don't do that." He would always say, "Let me know how that goes for you when you grow that third arm." Okay. But, like, I haven't grown a third arm. It's been a year. When am I going to grow that third arm? How long do I have to wait before this so-called consequence happens? When you get coronavirus, you don't need to wait that long for that consequence. If I weigh my options, a shot that makes me feel sick for a day is a lot better than brain damage or lung damage or, as you're saying, nerve damage.

Heart damage, nerve damage. Whatever goodwill I had in The Dalles from winning *Jeopardy!*, I spent every last bit of that trying to convince people to get vaccinated. I was on the front page of the paper twice. I talked about the Pfizer clinical trial and tried to convince anyone who might listen to get vaccinated. I did it to where I overstayed my welcome. I was active on hometown Facebook community groups until I got banned, not because I said anything that was wrong or even mean—

They didn't want to hear it.

They did not want to hear it.

I always wonder what it's going to take for some people to just kind of open their eyes and be like, "Oh, this is something I need to be careful about." For some people, it's their own life. Some people take that with them to the grave, that stubbornness. "Hey, I ain't getting that shot. It's from the devil." And then you see "I got sick, I'm going to be off Facebook for a while, couple days. Oh, I'm not feeling so well. I could use your thoughts and prayers next week." Then they're dead. It's sad. It's sad in a dumb way.

Just tell the truth. Tell the truth. I guess the overarching thing is that there's been a war on truth. Truth needs to be defended. It doesn't just take care of itself. You think it would, but it doesn't. All of what I wrote on Facebook, I stand by that. I did my utmost.

Inspiration 18

Let the truth pick your tribe. Never let your tribe pick the truth.

Don't let yourself believe falsehoods to fit in. Truth is a magnet for good people. It doesn't matter where you all started, truth will pull you together. Follow truth. See who else joins you. Truth will show you your tribe.

Inspiration 17

When we disagree with science, we're probably wrong.

In matters of faith, too often our own understanding is limited. On top of that, we may not understand the science. If you stop to think about it, what's more likely? Is it more likely that a thousand scientists are all wrong about their own field? Or is it more likely that we don't 100% understand how the universe works?

Doc Nukem

February 2, 2023

Today I met with Dr. Hope's younger colleague, Doc Nukem, my radiation oncologist. [2] Her lair is in the bowels of the cancer center past a ship's bell that patients ring on their last day of radiation. Doc Nukem walked me through my upcoming treatment. She will scan me while I am in some sort of body cast. Then she will irradiate me daily. The radiation will have to be spot on, or it will kill healthy organs. If chemotherapy is the poison gas blanketing my body's battlefield, radiation is the death ray that will burn out any survivors.

But what will Doc Nukem aim at? My CT scan was clear: I have no tumors above BB size. So what will be her target? She said she would aim at what's left of my

---

[2]I have to apologize to Doc Nukem. I was stuck when trying to come up with a pseudonym. So I asked her what name she wanted me to use. "Lady in Red." She said it without a pause. Doc Nukem likes red. She's worn it each time I've met with her. Her red dresses and scarves stand out among the Duke blue that is everywhere at the hospital. Lady in Red, I'm sorry—not enough sorry to go with Lady in Red, I'll note—but I am sorry. "Doc Nukem" made me laugh. I have cancer. I get privileges.

stomach and surrounding lymph nodes.

Doc Nukem, as I recalled from our initial meeting before chemo, is smart. More than that, she is confident enough to stop and think. I have interviewed thousands of doctors over my years as a consultant. I have had hundreds of pharma and biotech clients, often drawn from their companies' C-suites: chief executive officer, chief operating officer, chief financial officer, chief marketing officer, chief medical officer—lots of chiefs. They are all smart. They know they are smart. They are too smart not to know they are smart. They have enough ego to believe they are the smartest person in the room (as they often are). I find one trait separates the merely genius from the masters and mistresses of the universe. The thing that separates the best of them from the others is humility. The most successful, in my observation, have enough humility to keep learning despite their success. The learners stand out. The standouts have enough humility to be delighted to learn they are wrong even while their pride is pricked. The new thing, the thing that defied their expectation, that's interesting to them. They jump on their mistakes—not to cover them up but to learn something they didn't yet know.

Doc Nukem is like that. I saw it. She perked up when she realized on our first meeting that my pathology report wasn't the death sentence it had seemed on first read. I watched her pause, rewind, and—smile in her eyes—realize she was wrong. *Now isn't that interesting?* It played across her face as she registered that my case was a bit more unusual than that of yet another cancer patient sent to her because there was nothing better to do.

Doc Nukem's humility bought a lot of credibility with me. At the times when she told me I was wrong, I knew it wasn't because her ego was in the way. In my mind, my stomach remnant—the pouch that was left behind after my gastric bypass—was unrelated to my stomach cancer. My cancer was in the bypassed part of my stomach. The bypassed part wasn't hooked up. That was the point. There was no direct connection between my separated stomach parts. How would the cancer spread from one to the other? In my mind, my remaining stomach was the sun and my bypassed stomach the earth. Yes, they started as the same stuff. What of it? It's 2023. It's been over a decade since they were together. Doc Nukem reminded me that there are lymph nodes, and one lymph node of mine had been cancerous. Oh. Oh, yeah. Oh, crap.

I knew this stuff, once. But I hadn't thought it through. Sometimes white blood cells wander through tissue. More often white blood cells orbit organs like asteroids orbit the larger bodies of the solar system. White blood cells flow through lymph vessels and park in lymph nodes surrounding each organ. These are the lymph nodes that Dr. Z would have removed if he had known I had a gastric adenocarcinoma, not a GIST. Where white blood cells go, cancer follows. These same lymph nodes and the vessels that connect them can traffic cancer cells from one part of an organ to another, and later from one organ to the next. So if my cancer spreads anywhere—or has already spread—it will be in my remaining lymph nodes and remaining stomach remnant. This is why Doc Nukem wants to target it all.

She wants to be aggressive with the radiation. I'm young (well, for a cancer patient). I'm healthy (well, except for the cancer). The first shot at my cancer is the best one we will have. She didn't say it was the only shot we will have, but if my cancer spreads, the statistics say this shot is really the only shot at a cure.

She did warn me that the radiation could have long-term effects. I'll be at higher risk for melanomas or other new cancers. Radiation weakens everything it shines upon. My remaining stomach and the parts of my intestine in the path of the beam may rupture at some future date. That, I recall, is similar to what happened to the movie critic Roger Ebert. His irradiated coronary artery burst suddenly. However long I live, I will be at risk for intestinal bursts and blockages—weak pipes after cleaning.

She also warned me that we are stepping into the evidence-free treatment zone.

"There aren't good data for your kind of cancer," she said. I can't say I like working from theory when it comes to cancer. So much ends up being counterintuitive in practice, at least when it comes to chemotherapy. But that's the state of the art. Doc Nukem has to wing it. I'm choosing to trust her judgment.

After I left the hospital, I realized something had been nagging me without it quite breaking the surface of my thoughts. Remember how my stomach cancer wasn't seen on CT at first? The whole wall of my stomach was infiltrated by my diffuse gastric cancer, but on my first CT scan—the one that kicked all this off last summer when I was trying to donate my kidney—that part of my cancer wasn't seen. "Not appreciated"—that's how the pathologist put it. My first CT scan spotted my kidney tumor. My first CT scan saw the tumor outside my intestine. The part that was in my stomach? No. The part in my stomach was diffuse, sneaky, invisible to CT.

So how do we trust this new CT scan? Have I breathed a sigh of relief like a character in a horror movie? Has my cancer already spread more than just microscopically? Are we even aiming at the villain?

I messaged Doc Nukem the next day.

> How does one track the progression of a diffuse gastric adenocarcinoma with a CT scan? I'm just trying to get a handle on how you see something spreading if it's not mass-forming. Indirectly through cell-wall thickening and the like? Wait for differentiated masses? I'm also thinking how the gastric cancer wasn't seen, really, on CT initially other than the mass-forming portion that was on the duodenum.

She messaged me back:

> Diffuse type does not show up on PET/CT. Truthfully all imaging tests for this subtype are suboptimal and imperfect and CT scans are the best we have—for now at least.

Well, better to know.

Inspiration 16

Your memory is not as good as you think.

My memory is excellent. Your mom has the best memory of anyone I know. Both of us misremember all the time. If it can happen to us, it can happen to anyone. It's one thing when we forget something. That's not the worst of it. The worst is when we remember something that never happened. False memories feel exactly the same as real memories. We can't tell the difference, and you can't either.

Inspiration 15

Buy term life insurance.

Many things are called life insurance. The one you want is term life insurance. Term life insurance pays out if you die early and pays nothing if you live a long life. All other life insurance boils down to term life insurance plus overpriced investment. You don't need a complicated investment on the side.

I maxed out term life insurance as soon as I could afford the policy. I'm glad I did. What I bought for myself was peace of mind. I'm not spending my time these days worrying about how you kids and your mother will survive. What I bought was space for the family to live if I don't.

Body Bags

February 10, 2023

When you're getting radiation, you don't want the beam to miss. So Duke made me a full body cast of a sort. The cast will encase me as the radiation splits my DNA into millions of tiny pieces. I will need to be in exactly the same spot each radiation day. The radiation techs told me my body cast would be like a bean bag.

Every other imaging scan I've had was in an office lighted like the white room in *Willy Wonka and the Chocolate Factory*—the room where Mike Teavee is split into millions of tiny pieces and sent through the air by the power of Wonkavision. The bright light shines off the white floor, the white walls, the white gurney, the white machine.

In the radiation room, the lighting was low. It was dark. It was peaceful. The room is underground so stray beams don't hit anything or anyone vital. I was told to strip to my shorts and lie on the bean-bag body cast. The body cast was black. It didn't look like a bean bag. It looked like a body bag.

The body bag was full of tiny Styrofoam beads. The techs had me lie down with my arms above my head. I held that pose while they semi-buried me by pushing the bag with the Styrofoam beads against my sides. The beads felt like something between beach sand and the playground pebbles I used to burrow into at my elementary school in The Dalles. Once the radiation techs judged me to be sufficiently buried, they turned on a vacuum pump. The vacuum collapsed my body bag. The beads hugged me close. It felt surprisingly comfortable. I felt surprisingly comforted. I could get used to this—well, except for my neck. The beads pressed the top of my head and jammed my neck. The techs stopped the vacuum and reinflated the body bag so I could excavate more space for my skull. I wanted to get it right. This will be my resting place for twenty-five days. After three rounds of rearranging and re-inflating, I gave up. I will just feel a bit out of place. Oh, well. Nobody promised cancer would be comfortable.

As I dressed, the techs shelved my body bag in racks deep in the radiation room. Up to ten bags are stored there. Each one holds the shape of a person. The racks have all the charm of a morgue.

Oh, before the radiation techs extracted me from my body bag, they inked black and green alignment targets on my chest. I couldn't see what the techs were doing, but they pressed pretty hard. They left stickers over my ink and gave me instructions not to scrub the stickers off in the shower. The kids thought the ink looked like prison tattoos.

I started to wonder if my radiation techs might have given me actual tattoos under the ink—tiny ones—without informing me. Friends who have had cancer said they still have their radiation tattoos, each the size of a pinprick. Were my stickers to protect tattoos while the stain set? I suppose it would be in the tradition of a first tattoo to have no clear memory of the event. Still, did they really tattoo me without asking? I felt violated. I messaged Doc Nukem. She got back to me quickly.

> Historically tattoos were used and that system has been replaced at Duke with paint marker. The stickers are solely to protect the paint marker marks from water/friction, etc. We moved away from a tattoo system about 10–15 years ago.

It took me a surprisingly long time to let go of my false feeling of violation. I still think of the ink as prison tattoos.

My body bag will hold me still under the radiation beam. I won't be able to stop the movements of my breathing or pulse, but Doc Nukem believes she can get accurate-enough targeting with my body held firm.

I get my first dose of high-energy radiation in two weeks.

Inspiration 14

You only think you're a human polygraph.

You aren't good at detecting a liar. Essentially, nobody is. You probably don't believe me. But it's been shown over and over. We think we are good at spotting liars. We aren't. Instead, we default to trust. We trust people until inconsistencies build up. Only then do we see liars for what they are. Warning: It's embarrassing to admit, even to ourselves, that we have been taken in. Victims can be the most loyal defenders of con artists. Have compassion for those who are taken in by liars. That includes you.

Inspiration 13

If you want in the game, hang out at the court.

Success usually takes more than hard work and talent. There is also luck. Your classmate was in the loan department. Your friend knew of an opening not yet on the job boards. You reminded a powerful mentor of her granddaughter. The head of corporate communications heard your presentation the same day a conference speaker called in sick. This kind of luck doesn't just happen. You have to hang around the court if you want to be put in the game. The career equivalent is living in cities, attending schools, or choosing jobs alongside those who could elevate you. An internship at company headquarters could create this kind of luck. My summer job at Dunkin' Donuts never could.

If someone else gets a big break, then that position opens up for you to fill . . . if you are there, in plain sight.

Jump, Slip, Run Around

February 13, 2023

I have good news: Sam the Statistician is alive! I got an email from him today. He hadn't called me or responded to email earlier because he'd been hospitalized for Covid. He's out now but weak. Covid damages the heart. I gather it may have damaged his. I asked him to call when he feels up to it.

In our phone calls since my diagnosis, Sam has ended by telling me, "Jeff, you're not allowed to die." Sam is sweet. It's selfish of me, I know, but I'd really rather not outlive anyone I care about, including Sam. I'm filled to the brim with curiosity to see what happens after my own death. I'm a wimp when it comes to the death of others.

I think that's why I was so on edge throughout the pandemic. I found it hard to get distance from the deaths my training told me must come. My own mortality seems easier. My possible death is only really hitting my emotions now. I'm reading *Watership Down* to Annelise. I choke up at inappropriate moments. I catch myself thinking, *What if this is the last book?*

While we lived in Los Alamos, we took a family drive through New Mexico's mountains. We got stuck behind a pickup truck on a two-lane road that wound through piñon pines and rocks the color of meat. In the back of the pickup was a chained dog, big one.

When I was growing up, we drove many times with our dogs in the back of our pickup truck on the highway. Dogs in pickup beds are usually safe. They sometimes move around, but they keep low. Not this one. This dog started jumping up on the pickup's side panel, then slipping back in the truck bed.

The owners didn't seem worried. The dog must do this all the time, I thought. Jump, slip, run around. Jump, slip, run around. Jump, slip—

The dog jumped too far. It slipped but not back inside the pickup bed. The dog went over the truck side. The dog was still chained. It hit the ground and started spinning like a kind of chained-dog fur ball. It looked like the spinning Tasmanian Devil but on its side.

It was the most horrific thing I've ever seen.

The pickup stopped. The owners jumped out. The obviously injured dog ran off trailing its now-broken chain.

Jump, slip, run around. Now I'm the dog.

I haven't yet faced what my death would mean for the kids. I'm starting to catch a glimpse of it though. Most of the kids haven't had a death confront them. Jordan and Patrick did with Rod, Jennifer's brother. The five other kids, no. All four grandparents are alive. We've never kept a warm-blooded pet, so the kids haven't had the inoculation of smaller deaths to prepare them for a big one.

My father's mother died when I was in the fifth grade. Emotionally, it was the dividing point of my childhood. Before Grandma's Death. After Grandma. The B.G.D. years could be seen for what they were only once they were gone. I found myself in the world of the A.G. I didn't like it. Grandma Stewart had doted on me whenever I visited her in Portland. We watched television together when I wasn't outside playing or "helping" my grandfather with his firewood business. Grandma Stewart and I watched all the afternoon game shows and *Perry Mason*. We closed each day with the ten o'clock news. I kissed her dead lips in her coffin. She had been painted with pale lipstick in death I never saw her wear in life. It tasted of chalk. Afterwards, I kept a white ribbon from her funeral flowers in my closet. The ribbon sat next to *Axis & Allies,* one of the board games I played against myself.

I want to believe that my death won't divide my kids' lives the way Grandma Stewart's did mine. But how could it not? It will be worse. I want to believe my death will just be space for them—fresh air, new horizons, room to grow. I don't want to believe it will be the worst thing that has ever happened to them, perhaps will ever happen to them. I haven't yet looked in the eyes all that I must do for them.

Instead, I have found this one thing to do, and I am doing it. I write. I write to live. I write to avoid.

I loved my other grandmother too, my mother's mother, the one who lived in The Dalles and who listened to televangelists, but it was not the same. She was consumed with regret over the sure fate of my eternal soul. She feared for anyone who hadn't declared Jesus Christ to be a personal Lord and Savior. "Mormon Jesus" didn't count. Our conversations were dominated by warnings of the eternal pain of the Lake of Fire. She spoke from love. I could tell. Her death came when I was in college, married, with one child, and with the next on the way. She died of cancer. I was glad to have the excuse not to attend her funeral—not because I was resentful. I didn't want to grieve.

I haven't had a comfortable relationship with death. I have had an avoidant one. I think all of life is growing up. I sense some growing I still have to do. I may soon have to grow enough to sit with my kids in their anguish. I may not be able to avoid it for long, I think. Or at least I shouldn't. Am I hurting them now by being cavalier about cancer, for laughing and encouraging their *Breaking Bad* jokes?

I'm tearing up at the deaths of fictitious rabbits, for heaven's sake. I'm scared. I'm not scared of death. I think I'm scared of this part of living.

Inspiration 12

When we get why we kick the dog, we don't kick the dog.

Sometimes we choose to hurt ourselves or others. We can feel out of control. Why did I do that? It's the right question. Why *did* you do that? You did it because you got something out of it. Part of you liked it. That's hard to admit. Find the benefit you got from lashing out, from self-harm, from indulgence. When we uncover the benefit we got from hurtful acts, we can usually find a better way to meet our needs.

Inspiration 11

A list is the procrastination slayer.

If you're like me, jobs that can be done "whenever" are trouble. When there is no due date, I procrastinate. I work in sprints. If you are a serious procrastinator, your best career will be all sprints. Consulting is close to that. Every project comes with an insane deadline. I have no choice but to focus. To keep myself out of trouble when jobs don't have a real deadline, I have learned to set fake deadlines. I break the job down into small steps. I draw up a list. Then, before I can decide to do something else, I turn on my work-music loop and do the easiest item on the list. The starting is the hard part. Once I start on my list, I don't want to stop. I don't have to decide to keep working. I have my list.

Beam On

February 23, 2023

I started radiation today. What did radiation feel like? Radiation felt like nothing. At least, it felt like nothing at first.

Doc Nukem had told me what to expect. I am to come each day for radiation therapy. I can leave my car in valet parking, soak up my daily radiation dose, and take off in about an hour. I will be able drive myself home. I will probably feel fine the first treatment. Radiation won't make me radioactive.

Short term, radiation isn't too bad.

The techs led me into my radiation room. Outside, above the door, is a sign that reads "BEAM ON." The sign was off when we walked under it but can light up the way *Jeopardy!* studios had an "APPLAUSE" sign. BEAM ON warns the radiation techs to stay out of my room. They monitor me through closed-circuit television. Radiation is a monogamous relationship between the patient and the beam. No threesomes. Only voyeurs.

In the radiation room, I found my body bag waiting to clasp me. My bag was on the scanning table, but the machine behind it was not a familiar CT scanner with its huge doughnut. The radiation machine looks different from what I had expected. Honestly, the radiation machine looks like a giant KitchenAid mixer—the mixer that my parents gave us before Carissa was born and that sits on our kitchen counter today. The beam gantry loomed over my body bag just as the KitchenAid motor looms over the mixing bowl. The radiation will shoot out where the beaters would normally be. My stomach is what will be beaten.

Green lasers crisscross the beam room. These lasers align every important object in the room: the table, the beam, the body bag, me. I counted three lasers recessed in the walls and one right above the body bag that will line up to my fake prison tattoos.

The techs had me strip my shirt off. I could leave on my belt. The techs helped me clamber atop the table and cocoon myself in my body bag. They did let me push out another half-centimeter of head space so my neck wouldn't be compressed. That was a relief. The radiation techs body-Englished me as though they were pinball wizards who knew how much to shove the cabinet so the game doesn't tilt. I couldn't see my chest. The body bag held my head in place, and that place wasn't where I could see ink. I could look only straight up at the ceiling.

A small planetarium is set into the ceiling of the beam room. That, at least, gave me something to watch during radiation. The planetarium shows a blue sky with clouds and a scattering of LED stars. The planetarium sky cycles from day to night every few minutes. But the stars and clouds never move. There is no moon.

The beam gantry—the central part of the KitchenAid mixer the size of a love seat—whirred into place. The radiation techs left me to the beam, the stars, and Billy Joel playing "Uptown Girl" over the loudspeakers.

The beam started on a scanning mode. The gantry rotated around me slowly to build up an X-ray image of my bones, my guts, my chemo port, and my stomach. The whole KitchenAid gantry wound around to my right and out of sight. The gantry can shoot me from any angle.

In the room outside BEAM ON, Doc Nukem's minions reviewed today's scan. They confirmed that the radiation program—the one Doc Nukem had designed sometime in the preceding two weeks—was still lined up with my stomach this afternoon. I guess they were satisfied, because with a thunk and a low-budget *Doctor Who* ray-gun sound, the beam powered on.

There was nothing to see. The X-ray beam is a light that is bluer than blue. It's bluer than ultraviolet. It's bluer than normal chest X-rays. It's so blue our eyes can't see it. But it's bright, and it burns.

Inside the beam gantry, electrons were pushed along a particle-accelerator tube by a standing radiofrequency magnetic wave. Each wave gave the electrons a push as they passed through. Each push sped the electrons along like a child pushed on a merry-go-round by malevolent teenagers. Each push added up. The electrons raced faster and faster. By the time the electrons were flung from the end of the accelerator, they approached the speed of light. The electrons flew so fast that, as Einstein predicted, time slowed down, and the electrons' mass ballooned. Flying BBs became flying bullets massing twenty times what they had when they entered.

In the gantry, the part aimed at my stomach, those super-massive, super-fast electrons slammed into a plate of tungsten, the same metal found in older light bulbs. When tungsten is hit by electrons going nearly the speed of light, things happen. A brilliant flash of high-energy X-rays spewed from the tungsten into my stomach.

The beam circled around me at a measured pace. Billy Joel kept playing through the wail of high-voltage transformers. Metal plates set like teeth around the tungsten X-ray emitter opened and closed like a living thing, shaping the beam. As the beam swung to my front, the metal mouth opened wide to send its brightest blast into my stomach. X-rays poured into me and created unstable chemicals that ripped apart my DNA everywhere the beam landed.

Every day we get some radiation. We catch a few cosmic rays. We may walk past granite, which is slightly radioactive. Stray atoms of radioactive radon gas float from the earth we step on. It's not much. Usually, nothing bad happens. When something bad does happen, our DNA-repair proteins clean up the mess.

I looked up how much radiation I absorbed from treatment. Today and each day I have radiation therapy, I absorb the daily radiation I'd normally get over six hundred years. If a Henry the Fifth-sized bottle were hidden in the hedgerows of Normandy from when his longbowmen marched until now, and that bottle stored radiation, that's how much went into my stomach today. If a Jeff-sized bottle stored up radiation from the last Ice Age until today, that's how much radiation will flood my stomach before Doc Nukem is done. It's a lot.

But today I felt only a light sunburn.

Doc Nukem told me to expect fatigue to set in as we go through these weeks of treatment. Each radiation session will burn more of my reserves. I can also expect nausea. These unpleasantries will pass. I will recover my energy after radiation is done. My stomach will settle down once its lining of dividing cells isn't killed off each day (except weekends).

It's the permanent damage that makes me think *oh, boy*. Radiation isn't just killing my cancer. Radiation isn't just killing my gut lining. Radiation is also burning out some of the small blood vessels that keep my organs alive. Radiation is killing off stem cells that repair organ damage. It's a worry for another day, another year, another life.

I find it depressing—the never-ending task, not the difficult-but-quick problem to solve. If I were a family of one, I would choose *quick*. I would wager that my cancer is already dead. I wouldn't lie on this table for five weeks and take in fifteen thousand years of radiation. But I'm not a family of one. So I choose a chance at a longer—but possibly more painful—life.

Inspiration 10

Multitasking is a myth.

Attention is a spotlight. We can shine our light on only one thing at a time. There is no such thing as multitasking. There is only task switching. Task switching is slower than getting one thing done at a time. When we switch tasks, we also make mistakes. Those who say they are good multitaskers are the worst at it. I don't know why that is, but there have been serious studies showing exactly this.

Inspiration 9

Don't be afraid to chase a new dream.

Rock star is a dream career, right? It's not a good dream. It's a nightmare. Rock stars die twenty-five *years* too early. Filling stadiums with adoring fans is one of the worst pieces of bad luck that could ever happen to us. What other dreams are nightmares? The average baseball draftee earns only about half of what his childhood neighbors make. NFL players have three years of average play and twice the risk of early onset Alzheimer's, Parkinson's, and dementia. A year after the lottery, big winners are no happier and need a bigger thrill to feel normal—they take less pleasure in normal life.

Second-grade Jeff thought *Gilligan's Island* was super funny. Why should I trust *that* guy to pick my dream job?

You've grown taller. You can see the hidden garden over the brick wall now. You can also see the droppings on top of the car roof. Don't be afraid to chase a new dream. Be afraid not to.

This Estuary of Time

March 14, 2023

I'm not going to lie. Radiation plus chemo is kind of a drag.

Each week I take over one hundred pills:

- Thirty as chemotherapy
- Fourteen for nerve damage pain
- Seven for diarrhea
- Fourteen for nausea
- Seven to lower my stomach acid
- Seven to keep my hemoglobin levels up
- And twenty-two pills unrelated to my cancer treatment

I need them. I've been having my side-effect moments.

You know that feeling of too-rich food just sitting in your stomach? I feel that way all the time. Eating makes me feel as if I'm retraumatizing my radiation-weakened stomach. I am. Even soda on the drive home from treatment is a bit of a gut punch. Eating much of much knocks me out. I'm sleeping at all hours again. My menu list is getting shorter every day. I'm almost down to bread and ramen noodles. After radiation treatment, I vomit if I try to eat pizza with toppings. A sensible man would skip pizza. I'm not always sensible. I enjoy the pizzeria-and-podcast experience too much. I try to slip in my pizzeria run before the time window closes on the two hours before treatment, when I must fast.

Then this happened on my first and only day back in the office in the three years since Covid flooded our shores:

Well, that was fun. I crapped my pants all the way onto the chair at the company meeting.

Patrick

Yikes >_<

dad really didnt want an office job...

P

I don't know how many kids' onesies I've scrubbed out by hand over my years. A lot. Now I'm the child. I have compassion for myself. I see my kids in me. Losing control of bodily functions is the most human thing. Cleaning up a mess that can't wait has a clarity to it. There is no wishing it away. Waiting would make things worse. There is nothing for it but to act. Cleaning up crap is my kind of problem. Metaphorically.

My ability to work is fading from me. The three parts of my job are doing, managing, and selling. Of those, I love *doing* the best and *selling* the least. I'm valued in exactly the opposite order. I've had to let go of the things I love best about work. I'm no longer analyzing prescription drug data or scientific papers. I'm not interviewing physicians or hosting the company podcast. I'm relying on my managers to run my projects. I still sell. I've already made my sales target for the year. From my boss's perspective, I must seem to be doing more than ever.

I'm looking forward to the end of the month, the end of radiation, the end of chemo—hopefully for the rest of my life. My cancer may already be extinct. But if the cancer were to survive, I can't expect a long life.

I want to go home. This summer I plan to return to The Dalles. I can't help but wonder if it's for the last time. The Columbia River that flows past The Dalles is a highway for salmon. Salmon are birthed in fresh water, in the shallowest of streambeds. Salmon leave the small waters to grow strong in the sea and return at the end to the waters that birthed them. The Dalles will always be my home. I don't ever feel so solid as when I look out across the cherry trees and hills the color of wheat. No shapes are so firmly fixed in my mind as the horizons of my youth. Each ridge on the edge of the cloudless Eastern Oregon sky is as familiar to me as my wife's silhouette. Changes of the past half-century stand out to my eyes as fresh tattoos on a familiar face—new houses, saplings now grown, the missing water tower that was once painted in Purina-logo red and white, the scrawl of the now-paved road.

Of course, the river of my youth was not my forever place. It never could have been. In truth, the sea was not my place either. My place has been the between place, the estuary where the fresh water meets the salt. All my best ideas have taken two truths from different environments and put them together in a new way. Autoimmunity plus calico cats. Financial valuation plus clinical trials. Proteins plus haptics. The estuary is ever-changing. The problems are never quite the same. The changes stress fish better suited to the river or to the sea. I feel a sense of loss for those who never feel the slap of the waves. I laugh at the great whites who will never taste the fresh headwaters.

I see now that this era—the one that started with electric typewriters and ended with artificial intelligence—has been my place. I see now, looking back, how perfectly set I have been, like an irregular stone in the right ring. I can't know for sure there is a God, but if so, I smile to see how fondly he has placed me in time.

When it's my time to go, I'll miss this estuary of time. But I don't wish to relive it. I'm ever so curious to see what's next.

Inspiration 8

Food is cheap.
Healthcare is expensive.
Don't clean your plate.

I know it feels as if we are wasting money when we toss food in the trash. Let's be honest. It is. You know what wastes more money? Diabetes. You aren't in the seventh year of famine under Pharoah. If you're full, don't keep eating. You're not really saving money if you swallow food your body doesn't need. Don't force yourself to clean your plate.

Inspiration 7

Say *yes* to new things.

Part of being a child is saying *ew* to new foods. Grow up. We have a natural distrust of new things. Push past that. In your lifetime you will meet maybe one of the hundred thousand people best suited to be your bestest friend in the whole wide world. For every book you read, even if you read fast, another ten thousand will be published. Speaking of the whole wide world, you will visit at most only one in a thousand places in it. The best for you is out there. Give yourself a chance to find it.

I Like Playing Games

Layne: *It's a good thing you tried to donate a kidney.*

People need that kidney. The waiting lists are long. More than half of those on dialysis die within five years. Donation would cure them. And it's not as if you really give up much if you give up a kidney, to be perfectly honest. Your other kidney grows like a starfish. Cool, huh? There's pain involved, but the risk is basically zero. People who donate kidneys live *longer* than people who don't donate kidneys. Kidney donors are younger and healthier than average, but if you correct for age and health, the donation risk is zero.

It's safe?

It's safe.

I'm on chemo as we speak. I started chemo this week. Chemo sucks, but it's not as bad as the chemo other people get. It's a little bit easier regimen than, than some of the other chemo regimens.

You know, keeping the hair . . .

I'm keeping the hair. I'm not feeling great, but I'm keeping the hair. Chemo's making client meetings a little interesting, I have to tell you.

My prognosis is—I mean whoever listens to this I guess knows what happened—if progression happens, I'll have less than a year to live. If I survive for two years with no progression, I'll be basically clear. Psychologically, it's as if I live in two different worlds right now: the world where I'm dying, the world where I'm living. What do I want to do with the rest of my life? What priorities work with both of those outcomes? It's hard.

I never really thought about it like that. It must be almost surreal, in a way, to be, like, "Oh, this could be it . . . but also couldn't be." I guess that could be any day for anybody.

It's the human experience, in a way, but it is a lot more real these days. We should know in two years.

Hopefully, good news, right?

Hopefully. Even if it's bad news, even if it's not all right, it'll be all right one way or the other. I do feel bad about Jen and the kids, but I feel worse for my parents. I imagine that if any of my kids died oh, my gosh, it would just rip out my heart.

As you know, my grandma got cancer. She got that taken care of, but it came back, and she got the chemo. She lost her hair. But, man, that old woman, she had a little power scooter. She was riding around. We went to D.C. She still had all that life in her. To me it's, like, that's what's so essential. Like when you go to, what are they called? Like ICUs. I want to say hospice.

Infusion centers for chemo or hospice centers to die.

Not to die but to get chemo, so an infusion center. Just like when people are in a good mood and every time is a good time, you just feel like you don't want to be around people who are, like, "Aw, I'm sorry. Can we get the casket now?" Relax. We don't know yet. I think she had that type of attitude where she's like, "Don't worry about that. Don't worry about it. We'll get there. Let's just have fun now." That really carried with me for a long time. It was hard to me.

She was trying to protect you, don't you think?

To a degree. But even before that, she was always like that. She wasn't the richest person around. I mean real poverty. She tried her best, and my dad always says that it's not about the money. It's about the stuff you do for people. I think she was like that: "Don't worry about me." You know, she was a very powerful woman in that way. And I just . . . it's inspiring. So I think what you're doing now, not being so morose, not walking around with your little IV stand, you know, that type of stuff . . .

I got the oral regimen because I didn't want to have the IV stand here at the house. That would just be too much.

It's a little morale hit—like, oof. *I don't know if she wants me to speak on it, but you know, obviously for your kids, Jessica at least, I know she is a little worried, which, of course, naturally. Your mom's so funny. "Don't worry! He'll be fine!" But I think, well, she kind of has to be, right? Your mom's a very focused woman. It feels like she's always on the move. As you said with your dad, but your mom's the same way, they are very hardworking people. Your dad is hands-on, mechanic shop, do the farm, do the construction. I know your mom is different—the way she has to do her substitute teaching. When she's over here, she's cleaning the whole house. Just, like, really? What is she, seventy-three?*

She's seventy-seven turning seventy-eight.

When I'm seventy-seven, I'll probably be in a wheelchair, honestly. Just roll around, be like, "I can't do it." I'll enjoy my retirement. But yeah, it's inspiring to see people who can stay positive when, as you said, they're faced with the two options. It's a flip of a coin in a way.

This one just seems to be pretty binary. One thing I have learned about myself is that the stakes don't matter. It can be a little game. It can be huge game. It can be life and death. I just play it. I play. I like playing games.

Inspiration 6

Give one thing your all.

Climb the mountain. Master the instrument. Pour yourself into the subject. Hold nothing back. Spend yourself. See what that buys you. Push yourself at least once in life to be the best you can possibly be. The pushing will stretch you. It will show you what you can do. It will give you courage to fight lesser fights. When someone calls you less-than, you will look back and remember who you were when you gave it your all. Nobody can take that from you.

Inspiration 5

Do it until you are it.

We feel like frauds when our actions don't match our beliefs. When actions and beliefs fight, actions win. We change our minds. We justify. "What's the harm?" "It's not as if we had a contract." "They owed me." Cognitive dissonance—that fraud feeling—is not all bad. We can run that engine in reverse. We can choose to do the hard-but-right thing anyway. When we choose the hard-but-right act, our beliefs might whine about it for a while, but soon enough they sigh and get with the program. Our beliefs change for the better. Doing good changes us. Do it until you are it.

All Possible Worlds

There is a serious branch of physics that holds there is not just one universe. There are infinite universes. In a real way, as one version of the theory goes, we live every possible life, not just this one. We make different choices. Each choice we make, the universe splits.

If so, what am I? Am I the one Jeff stuck in this one reality, the one set of choices I've made? Or am I the sum of Jeffs that made all the choices, good and bad? A subatomic particle takes every possible path. Some paths reinforce each other. Other paths cancel each other out. The final path we observe is the sum of histories. Will my bad choices collapse in destructive interference? Will my good choices reinforce and be the sum of me?

I have such regrets. You may laugh at some of these. You may shake your head at others. I hope I've learned from these mistakes. They still bother me.

It's show-and-tell in the second grade. My friend Wayne is showing off his plastic dinosaurs. He can't remember the name of one, so in front of the class, he asks me the right name. I answer. But I don't stop there. "Should I also say the names of the other ones you got wrong?" I know what I am doing. I am trying to seem high in front of others by pressing a friend down. This isn't the last time.

It's Princeton. I'm invited to a snooty dinner with a visiting Nobel laureate. One older professor from my department is trying to ingratiate himself. "Most people assume I'm in the National Academy, but I haven't been nominated yet." It's a cry from someone who fears being forgotten. It's transparent even to me. There, in the dining hall, the professor pulls out his published papers and hands them to the Nobel laureate. The professor makes a reference to Candide's having said "this is the best of all possible worlds." That's a trivia question. I know the answer. The professor is wrong. It wasn't Candide who said it. It was Dr. Pangloss in the same play. And Voltaire didn't believe the optimism but was satirizing it. I see my moment to inject myself in the conversation. I cut down, or think I cut down, the striving professor. I don't know what it's like to be near the end of your career and have some smart-aleck student take you down at a dinner party in front of your hero. I do know what it's like to do it. It didn't even feel good then.

It's Los Alamos, and Jen needs me. I want to play cards. She jumps on the car hood to keep me from leaving. I pull out of the driveway anyway. I probably won the card game.

It's Little League baseball in The Dalles. My team is at bat. The pitcher is Buffy. She's the only girl pitching in Little League. We start the chatter to distract her. I can hear myself saying the one thing I think will most rattle her. I had read it in a comic strip, *Peanuts*, I think. "Go home and do the dishes!" I jeer it at her one pitch. I do it the next. Are Buffy's parents in the stands? They must be. I shout it. I shout it because I want to win.

It's Princeton, and my labmate Michele has just published her first paper. She's beaming. She has the author copy in hand. I read her paper and find an error. I tell her I wish she had asked me to read the paper before submission. She turns red and tries not to cry.

I'm a mid-rank Boy Scout in The Dalles. I'm on a small board of review for a younger scout named GW. He hasn't memorized the Scout Oath he is required to for advancement past Tenderfoot. He's obviously nervous. Memorization is hard for him, and he knows it. He's scared. He's scared of me. I could let him off the hook and pass him. I could coach him through the "memorized" lines. I don't. Instead, I fail him. An adult leader takes over.

I'm off for the summer from BYU. I'm in the musical *Working* as part of a high school theater reunion production. I'm not given a featured song. It feels like high school all over again. My singing is dismissed by the same high school director. I ask my cousin Gary to give me his song. I can't believe how small I am to do that. I can't believe how large he is to do what he does. He gives me his song.

It's Princeton, and I'm breeding mice for genetic studies. Mice are expensive to keep. I have to kill most of them. I kill them in carbon dioxide because that's what we do. The mice don't die quietly. They jump and slam themselves against the top of the domed canister. I can hear them. I can see them through the plastic. I want to be doing good science. I know that I am depressed and am going through motions that aren't going to answer anything. I kill the mice anyway. I leave a note on the whiteboard about gassing mice like Nazis and sign it "Love, PETA." I think I'm going mad.

It's my MBA program. Jen learns her younger brother has died. I don't like funerals. I know the teachers would be understanding of my missing class. I could make up the work. I don't try. I let her travel by herself from South Bend to New Jersey. I let my wife face her family and her brother's body without me. She is six months pregnant with Mallory. Afterwards, I tell Jen to stop thinking about her brother. She suffers alone.

It's New Mexico, and I'm playing in a *Magic: The Gathering* tournament with my oldest son, Jordan. I'm randomly paired against him. He makes a mistake that will disqualify him from the game if a judge learns about it. I call the judge. Jordan tears up. The judge looks at me, the dad who wanted to win so much he got his son a game loss. Some lesson.

It's Chatham, New Jersey. Diane from church has stage IV breast cancer. I want to be seen as someone who knows something. I tell Diane the only thing I know—vaguely—about a new cancer treatment. It is for a different kind of cancer and is completely useless to her. I know right away that I'm probably raising hope where there is none. Thankfully, she can tell I don't know what I'm talking about.

I'm attending church in Los Alamos. A man named Bob introduces himself to the congregation. He's just moved across the country to work for the lab. He thanks the members for being attentive to his family's needs. He says that, in a previous congregation, the member who was supposed to minister to him—the one assigned to be his personal minister—never showed up. He says how thankful he is to have someone who actually cares about him and his family here. I realize as I look up that I recognize Bob. He is from Princeton. I am that assigned minister who never showed up.

There is a thread woven through my regrets. I have to lay the patches together to see it. I regret when I knew the right thing to do and didn't do it. That's the ugly side of the sewing. I also now see what's not there. I don't regret my honest mistakes. I have made many bad decisions. They were tuition. I learned from them. They don't haunt me. The mistakes that haunt are those where I knew better and didn't listen.

May I redeem myself a bit?

It's North Carolina. I'm assigned at church to minister to Pat. Pat is in a nursing home. Her body is failing. So is her mind. She can barely see. She lies in bed with the lights low and the curtains drawn. Her widescreen TV sits unplugged. She says she misses church and asks to be driven there. I'm not allowed. She tells me she wants to die. She prays for it. This time, I show up. I bring my internet hotspot so we can watch church broadcasts together. We talk about her family. She tells me about her life. I read her *Pride and Prejudice*. She remembers it from her childhood. I read her a chapter each visit. She stops telling me about praying to die. I show up until she catches a respiratory virus. We give her a blessing of comfort but not healing. Then she dies. She never remembers my name. I'm glad I didn't build a new regret for a change.

This cancer diagnosis has been a blessing. I'm so glad I got the diagnosis. The diagnosis may have saved my life. The greater blessing is if I die. If I die, the diagnosis gave me time. The diagnosis gave me the will to act. I have been blessed with time to prepare my family, to prepare myself. I have been blessed with the time and will to write this.

That's not where the blessings end. The greatest blessing is not just my early diagnosis. The greatest blessing has been the cancer itself. I'm glad I got cancer, all things considered.

I have been gifted the opportunity to share my cancer experience with others. They are reaching out. What a blessing it is to hold another's horrors for them. "I have told this to nobody but my priest and my wife." What a blessing it is to hear "this helped me understand what my mother went through." What a blessing it is to calm fear of the unknown. What a blessing it is to sit with someone going through the worst thing in their life. Cancer is frightening, confusing, overwhelming. Explaining my cancer gives new purpose for this time in this life of mine. Explaining my cancer breathes fresh meaning into the learnings and the failures of my life.

I couldn't have written this without cancer. So thank you, cancer, for being there. I hope to live to do more, but if the price I pay to do some good is you, your price is cheap.

Inspiration 4

Put your best foot back.

When we are strong performers in one area, we feel comfortable focusing on that. If we write dialogue well, we like to think about dialogue. We feel safe spending our effort on what we do well. We put out best foot forward.

Putting our best foot forward is not always the best approach. If we really are great at something, that part will take care of itself. Instead of leading with your best foot, put your best foot back. Focus your attention on where you feel unsure. Give your attention to your weak spots. Obsess over your plot. Your dialogue will still flow. You'll usually end with a better result.

Inspiration 3

Do the job right, and you don't have to look back.

A job done wrong nags at us. When we do a job right, we can be bold. We don't keep looking behind us. When I repaired radiators in your grandfather's shop, I made sure every bolt was tight. I never regretted that, even if it meant some late nights. It's easier to sleep well when we know we did the job right.

Ring the Bell

March 29, 2023

This was my last day of therapy. I've been looking forward to this. Mostly. These past few weeks have been my hardest. My white blood cells are low. So are my platelets. I'm so tired. Rest doesn't rejuvenate. Rest just keeps me from feeling so . . . done.

My family asked me how I would be celebrating. So did the radiation techs. I'm not one who likes a lot of fuss. I just want to sleep it off. Honestly, the part about today I've been dreading the most has been ringing the bell outside the radiation suite—the ship's bell that announces to everyone in the waiting room that I am done with therapy. I've seen that twice over the past five weeks while waiting for my beam room to free up. The bell rings. Everyone claps. I like applause fine. I just like it to be for something I've done on stage, not something done to me on a table.

I should have made more of my moments rather than just shutting down and waiting for treatment to get over. I slowed down as though that would help time speed up. It didn't. Einstein lied.

One thing that has buoyed me during cancer has been a dream I had years before.

This one stuck with me. I dreamed I died. I don't recall ever dreaming that before. The dream taught me something about myself. The dream—like most dreams—had a nonsensical setup. Jen and I were driving. But we weren't in our minivan on the highway. We were in a convertible racing atop a giant platform raised hundreds, perhaps thousands, of feet in the sky. The platform was colorful, like a painted wooden toy. As I drove, I lost the track. I drove the car off the platform into the air. We were falling, my wife and I, in the car that rotated to see the ground, the sky, the ground, the sky. The ground raced toward us. I had at first the same feeling I had felt when the dog slipped from the pickup truck in New Mexico. There was nothing we could do. And we hit. My dream ended there. This wasn't a dream about heaven. I saw no afterlife. I felt no greater presence. The important part of the dream was what I felt as we fell, after I realized there was nothing, nothing I could do to stop it. We would die. And my life would be over. In my dream, I felt the horror fall from me. I didn't feel sick. I didn't feel a need to plead. I didn't feel as though I had been robbed. I was excited. I smiled at dream-Jen and thought, *That was quite a ride. I wonder what happens next?*

I don't know yet how I will die or when. I think I know how I will react. *That was quite a ride. I wonder what happens next?* I've been sitting on that comforting thought all through treatment. It's helped me all year.

But that bell has made me rethink.

The radiation techs were chipper. They always were. My last pass through the BEAM ON room was like my first—this time with Tom Petty and the Heartbreakers playing rather than Billy Joel. "Mary Jane's Last Dance" was my exit song as I emerged one final time from my body bag. The techs deflated my body bag. The shape of me faded away.

On my way out, I hadn't decided if I was going to ring the bell or not. I don't do ritual well. It seems silly. But I knew I would be writing this chapter. And "Ring the Bell" was just too good a title to leave behind.

I rang the bell.

Everyone clapped. "I'm outta here!" I called with a wave. I thought with that I could make my exit without any more bother.

"Congratulations, Mr. Stewart," said a voice I hadn't expected. It was a nurse whose name I hadn't bothered to commit to memory. I couldn't speak. I'm sorry, but I just couldn't. I could only nod. "Congratulations, Mr. Stewart," said the receptionist whose name I had remembered (Jada) since I saw her every day, and who would greet me by name before I showed her my ID. "Congratulations, Mr. Stewart." I started to cry. I didn't want to disturb the other patients by sobbing in a cancer center, so I tried to hold it together as I willed myself away.

That was stupid of me. They would have gotten it.

I don't know quite what was bottled in me. I don't know why a kind word uncorked it. But I cried all the way to the parking garage.

It's over. One way or the other, it's finally over. If the cancer is gone, I will have my port removed in a year. In two years, if there is no spread, I will live the rest of what I can expect to be a long life. If the cancer is not gone, I will not get radiation again. It will be too late for that. I will probably get more chemotherapy and a new treatment targeting the claudin 18.2 protein. These treatments will not save me. They cannot. They can delay death only by a few months. On my last treatment visit with Dr. Hope, I confirmed this. I asked her this straight. She closed her eyes to think and made a decision. "I like to say there is always hope," she said, "but you're right. We might get a few more months. But it won't cure you."

The truth is, when it comes to life, I don't know what I will feel when I ring the bell.

Inspiration 2

Wish everyone well.

I think we are closest to God when we wish everyone well. The line between Us and Them fades. Everyone starts to be in our family.

You'll see those who are led to the opposite path. They draw their border inward. They become smaller, meaner versions of themselves. The whole world becomes one big Them. That world is frightening.

How do we expand our borders and wish everyone well? We start small. We start with those we find it easy to love. We wish them to have the very best. We wish them to be their very best. We wish them well. Then we expand to those we find it less easy to love. We wish them well too. Then we expand to those we find it hard even to tolerate. We wish them well. Finally, we expand and wish everyone well. Social scientists tell us this process works. I didn't just make it up. Those same social scientists say this process helps us do good. We don't just feel better about others by wishing them well. We go out and make the world a better place.

Inspiration 1

Kindness is all that really matters.

It's nice to be smart. It's nice to be attractive. It's nice to be talented. None of that matters one bit if we aren't kind.

Some people open their homes, bring cookies, or give a big hug to anyone they already know. Their kindness is focused. They will give the shirt off their back to a friend. Others shine their kindness through a panoramic lens. They try to solve injustice, climate change, world hunger. Kindness is the light, and we are the lens. Here's the thing: Many of us practice using only one setting on our kindness lens. Some shirt-off-their-backers say hurtful things about foreigners. Some world-savers won't talk to members of their own family. The light of kindness can be plenty bright, but it's not always pointed everywhere it ought to shine. Before writing off anyone as heartless, check to see if the setting is stuck on their kindness lens. Encourage unsticking if you can.

Anyone can choose to be kind. Kindness is all that really matters.

Acknowledgments

Thank you, my wife, for being a well-matched companion for more than three decades. I'm so glad I met you. Thank you, my children, for being you; a father could want nothing more. Thank you, my parents and my teachers, for loving me into being. Thank you, my colleagues, for serving others alongside me. Thank you, my friends, for being true friends and for letting me be yours. Thank you, Dr. Hope Uronis, Dr. Manisha Palta, Dr. Michael Abern, Dr. Sabino Zani, and the rest of my cancer-care team, for treating me with kindness and for answering my many questions. Thank you, Kickstarter contributors, especially Meg Fitzgerald, for your generous gifts that helped me put my all into this work. Thank you, Jennifer Wadsack, Jill Bailin, Daniel Bodhaine, and Rose Green for contributing your time and talent to help birth this book. And thank you, Sam Litwin, Phil Seiden, Martin Weigert, Perry Watts, and Michele Shannon, for helping me emerge from a hard time.

Final Inspirations

If you or a loved one has received a cancer diagnosis, I'm sorry. I'm sorry this has happened to you. Cancer is frightening. It's all so complicated that, when we get the diagnosis, we don't know what to think. We barely know what to feel. Understanding cancer and its treatment—even the hard things to hear—helped me be less afraid. I hope, I pray, my story helps you even though your cancer, your experience, may be different from mine. I'm not going to pretend to be an oncologist and give treatment advice—listen to your oncologist—but if you need to talk, I'm at authorjeffreystewart@gmail.com. I'll respond if I'm able.

To my colleagues in the healthcare industry: There is an opportunity to do good here. The cancer patient needs a trusted, friendly voice to help explain things—on call, 24/7. The healthcare system isn't prepared to do this. The vacuum is filled now by fraud and fear. Cancer patients today are not in a neutral information environment. Instead, cancer patients are flooded with false facts and quacks who promise 100% cure rates. That's the reality we live in. There is one defense against misinformation that we know works: pre-bunking. We must fill cancer patients with facts in forms they can understand before the frauds get to them. How do we do this without hiring a call-center army of oncologists? I'm hopeful that artificial intelligence trained on the best evidence will be a "cancer counselor" that will be there to explain things to patients anytime, day or night. There is upside for us all: Patients who follow evidence-based medicine have double the chance of surviving their cancer. Demonstrating an AI cancer counselor has a positive effect on medication compliance *or even overall survival* in a clinical setting should be possible with a modest number of clinical-trial patients. The pieces are there. Done right, an AI cancer counselor could save more lives than many cancer treatments. If I survive my cancer, I hope to join you in the effort.

Jeff Stewart, April 2023

Photo credit Franklin Knox. Copyright © 2022. Used with permission.

Jeff Stewart is a healthcare consultant, scientist, inventor, award-winning playwright, and father of seven. He was a *Jeopardy!* College Champion and runner-up in the Tournament of Champions. Jeff lives in Cary, North Carolina.

Printed in the USA
CPSIA information can be obtained
at www.ICGtesting.com
LVHW041248230923
758576LV00001B/2